Single Women

Single woman is not just some cultural oddity. She is our future.

Jay Rayner, 'We want to be alone',
The Observer, 6 January 2000

Single Women:
Challenge to the Church?

Kristin Aune

paternoster
press

Copyright © 2002 Kristin Aune
This edition copyright © 2002 by Paternoster Publishing

08 07 06 05 04 03 02   7 6 5 4 3 2 1

Paternoster Press is an imprint of Paternoster Publishing,
PO Box 300, Carlisle, Cumbria CA3 0QS
and
Paternoster Publishing USA
PO Box 1047, Waynesboro, GA 30830-2047
www.paternoster-publishing.com

British Library Cataloguing in Publication Data
A catalogue record for this book is available from the British Library

ISBN 1-84227-115-6

Cover design by Diane Bainbridge
Typeset by WestKey Limited, Falmouth, Cornwall
Printed and bound by Omnia Books Ltd., Glasgow

Contents

Acknowledgements

This project began in 1998 as a dissertation for an MA in Women's Studies at the University of York. Thanks are due first to the Economic and Social Research Council for providing the funding for the MA. I am grateful to the members of the Centre for Women's Studies at the University of York and in particular to Myfanwy Franks for supervising the dissertation and to Ann Kaloski-Naylor for encouraging me to turn it into a book.

A number of people provided comments and other help. These included Emma Brewster, Steve Chilcraft, Claire Evans, Sheena Gillies, Marijke Hoek, Laura Jervis, Renée McMullen, Nick Pollard, Carrie Sandom, Professor Andrew Walker and Heather Wraight. Alison Hull's work in the commissioning stage was much appreciated. Thanks to my mother for thinking of the book title.

Special thanks to Martha Crossley for incisive proof-reading and insightful editing of the whole manuscript prior to submission.

I am grateful to my friends for their interest and encouragement.

Finally, my greatest debt is to the women who contributed to this book, either through letter writing, interviews or completing questionnaires. Without their help, this book could not have been written, and I would like to dedicate it to them.

Introduction

The summer of 2000 saw a debate rage on the pages of *Christianity* magazine. The June 2000 issue carried an article on the plight of single Christian women unable to find partners. The headline read:

> With more than double the number of single women attending church than men, thousands of Christian women are struggling to find a partner. What's a woman to do? Settle for a nerdy anorak, join an agency, date non-Christians or sit back and 'trust in the Lord?'

The article quoted several single women and directors of Christian dating agencies who all asserted that singleness was an unfortunate state to be escaped if at all possible. The overall message given out was that joining a dating agency was the only way to escape an unhappy single future.[1]

In August 2000, *Christianity* published a substantial selection of the letters it had received in response to the article, along with a contrasting piece on the situation of single Christian men. This article views the desperation of single women unhelpful, for 'men feel that women do not see them as just friends but as potential partners'. Its author, Nick Page, noted that 'throughout the church there is a subconscious and deep-rooted distrust of single men. After all, if they were serious about life they'd have got married, wouldn't they?' He went on to criticize the

---

[1] Lorraine Kingsley, 'Looking for Mr Right', *Christianity*, June 2000.

traditional Christian ideal of masculinity that delineates the ideal man as highly attractive, married, financially successful and involved in leadership within the local church, and concludes:

> What is needed, I think, is for the church to turn the pressure off. Instead of seeing young men as potential husbands and fathers, maybe we should start seeing them as human beings.[2]

Many of the published letters concurred with this viewpoint, criticizing the single women article for advocating a form of Christianity that seeks personal, romantic happiness rather than seeking to serve God, and for valuing single people according to their status as potential partners. One woman's letter concluded: 'Jesus is, after all, a pretty good role model for thirty-something singletons.' A *Christianity* columnist attempted to seal the argument, declaring that both articles had 'missed the point' and calling single Christians to 'resist the social trend of singleness' in order to promote 'family life'.[3]

Given that the proportion of single people in society as a whole is rising steadily, singleness is in urgent need of discussion and understanding by the church. For the society towards which the church has a mission is acutely touched by the issue of singleness. By 2010, over half of the UK population will be single. Yet singleness is becoming an increasingly complex state within society, as relationships form and dissolve along a spectrum which includes dating, cohabitation, marriage, divorce, separation and widowhood. Marriage and partnership are providing no easy solution to the dilemmas of life, and relationship breakdown is on the increase. Few of today's single people are, or want to be, single in the long term. For the younger generation, celibacy is an outmoded concept, and sexual relationships are a feature of singleness rather than its antithesis.

---

[2] Nick Page, 'Single Christian Man: an Endangered Species', *Christianity*, August 2000.

[3] Rob Frost, 'You got it Wrong', *Christianity*, August 2000.

In the church, singleness is also a major issue. Most significant is the gender imbalance among Christian singles. Single women form a quarter of adult church membership, in contrast to a single male membership of only a tenth. Living as a Christian single in a world in which singleness has come to take on very different and arguably unbiblical meanings, is becoming more and more difficult. Christian single people, along with their married counterparts, need to understand how to interpret, speak about and where necessary resist contemporary societal definitions of singleness. Because of the gender imbalance in the church, the burden of this has fallen to single women. Whether or not they desire marriage, few are able to find a Christian man to marry. The sheer number of them makes it necessary for them and for the rest of the church to think through the issues they face.

The *Christianity* debate was a microcosm of the evangelical church's 'problem' of what to do with its single people and, in particular, its single women. Do single women pose a threat to the 'family'? Are they social misfits desperate for a partner to make their lives complete? Are they self-possessed followers of Christ who value each other as fellow humans, rather than as sexual successes or failures? Or does the truth lie somewhere in between? Furthermore, are today's evangelical churches helping or hindering them in their service and worship of God? What is the church's attitude to their singleness and what opportunities for service does it allow single women? Most importantly, how can Christians address single women in a constructive and biblical way in order to further their involvement in the progress of the gospel?

This book began life as research on never-married evangelical women for an MA dissertation in 1998, during which time interviews were conducted with around a dozen never-married evangelical women. Half a dozen letter testimonies were also received from women, in response to an advertisement placed in *Woman Alive* magazine. Further questionnaire research in 2001 yielded responses from 76 never-married, divorced, separated and widowed women aged between eighteen and seventy-eight, bringing the total number of women involved in this research to 94.

Chapter 1 considers the state of singleness in contemporary society, before relating this to existing research on singleness in the church. Chapters 2, 3 and 4 reveal the results of this study on single evangelical women. Chapter 5 presents a theology of singleness, with particular reference to women. Chapter 6 contains recommendations for improving the treatment of single women within the church.

Although single Christian women can be shown to form a distinct category and to have some similar concerns, it is also true that each woman is as individual as anyone else who is categorized in one particular way. In this book are women whose views on and experiences of singleness, marriage, the church, dating and sexual issues are wide-ranging and often divergent. For every woman who views singleness in a positive light, there is another who regards it negatively. For every woman who loves her independence, there is another for whom independence is simply loneliness. For every woman who feels supported by her church, there is another who feels let down. One experiences singleness as liberating, one as restrictive. One wants children, one does not. One has little desire for sexual activity, while another struggles daily against temptation. What's more, understanding of biblical teaching on singleness and women differs extensively. Some women believe the Bible encourages women's singleness; others think it prefers women to marry. Some believe it advises women to serve God where they are now; others believe it is legitimate for them to look for a marriage partner first. Some believe single women should have equal access to all ministry opportunities within the church; others believe certain roles should be denied them.

In the light of such divergent beliefs, the differing views presented here are likely to be met with relief, criticism, joy, anger, engagement and frustration. Single evangelical women face precisely these contradictions. To be a single evangelical woman is to stand in an ambiguous position relative to understandings of marriage, womanhood and religious identity both within the church and within contemporary society.

1

Society

Singleness in UK society

In 2000, 32 per cent of British households were single-person households (29 per cent contained one person, and 3 per cent contained two or more unrelated adults). This represents a rise of 5 per cent since 1981. A further 9 per cent were occupied by a lone parent and his or her children; less than one in ten of these lone parents is male.[1] These single-person households represented a quarter of the population.[2] By 2010, the proportion of households headed by a single person is forecast to rise to 40 per cent.[3] The number of adults living with their parents is also increasing.[4]

Reasons for this increase in single people are varied. A report from the Henley Centre for Forecasting cites three reasons: increased affluence, the break-up of relationships and lower rates of marriage.[5] For women particularly, their relatively recent socio-economic independence from men means that they no longer need to be married in order to achieve a high standard of living. The reduced stigma attached to divorce, as well as

---

[1] Office for National Statistics, *Social Trends 30: 2000 Edition* (London: The Stationery Office, 2000), 37.

[2] Office for National Statistics, *Social Trends 31: 2001 Edition* (London: The Stationery Office, 2001), 42–3.

[3] Jay Rayner, 'We want to be alone', *The Observer*, 16 January 2000.

[4] Office for National Statistics, *Social Trends 30*, 47.

[5] J. Rayner, 'We want to be alone'.

changes in divorce laws, has meant that divorce is easier and more frequent, and greater social acceptance of cohabitation has reduced the number of marriages. Since 1970–71, the number of first marriages has halved, and the average age at first marriage has risen from twenty-four to twenty-nine for men, and from twenty-two to twenty-seven for women.[6] Furthermore, as people lose faith in the durability of permanent relationships and the emotional fulfilment they once promised, more are opting to stay alone. Fewer people see parenthood as a necessary stage in life and, for women, childlessness is becoming increasingly common. The Office for National Statistics predicts that 23 per cent of women born in 1973 will be childless at the age of forty-five.[7]

There are more single women in the UK than single men. In 1996–97, 41 per cent of women were single (22 per cent had never married, 12 per cent were widowed and 7 per cent divorced). For men, 38 per cent were single (28 per cent had never married, 4 per cent were widowed and 6 per cent divorced). While there are overall more single women than single men, there are wide variations according to age. Up to the age of forty-five, more men than women are single. Between the ages of forty-five and fifty-four the proportion is equal, and after fifty-four, there are more single women. These trends result from a number of factors: more male babies are born than females; men die earlier than women and men marry on average two years older than women. Also, 63 per cent of women aged over seventy-five were widows.[8] The Office for National Statistics predicts that true figures would show a higher proportion of single people, estimating that 48 per cent of women and 46 per cent of men were single in 1999.[9] If trends continue, by 2005 less than half the female population will be married.[10]

---

[6] Office for National Statistics, *Social Trends 31*, 47.
[7] Office for National Statistics, *Social Trends 30*, 44.
[8] Office for National Statistics, *Social Focus on Women and Men* (London: The Stationery Office, 1998), 12 and 10.
[9] Office for National Statistics, *Population Trends Winter 2000 No.102* (London: The Stationery Office, 2000), 50.
[10] Fiona Gibson, 'No Strings Attached', *The Observer*, 18 March 2001.

To measure singleness according to the number of people who are unmarried no longer provides an accurate statistic, due to the decline in the number of people marrying and the increase in cohabitation. In 1998–99, a quarter of non-married women aged between sixteen and fifty-nine were cohabiting, the largest percentage (39 per cent) occurring in the twenty-five to twenty-nine age group.[11] This figure is almost double that of 1986.[12] This means that the proportion of women who are single and not cohabiting is just below one third.

There is an additional problem with defining and measuring singleness. *Company* magazine explains:

> The truth is, these days, single can mean anything. Single can mean you've been living with someone for eight years. Single can mean you're engaged to a serial killer on death row, who you write to every day but have never met ... Most of the time ... we live in a woolly area that isn't quite single but can't really be called anything else.[13]

For those whom *Observer* journalist Jay Rayner terms the 'New Singletons', there is a 'remarkable shifting between the coupled and the uncoupled state' as people drift in and out of relationships.[14] The *Observer* panel called together to debate singleness in contemporary society were agreed on one thing: they did not know how to define singleness.[15]

In a society that sees marriage as of reduced significance, what matters is whether one is or is not partnered. To be single is often taken to mean that one is not currently in a sexual relationship. Such a 'relationship', in turn, may take on a more temporary quality. Kate le Vann, writing in *Company*, describes the 'Two-Week Relationship' as an observable social trend:

---

[11] Office for National Statistics, *Social Trends 30*, 40.

[12] Office for National Statistics, *Social Trends 31*, 45.

[13] Kate le Vann, 'So, you think you're single?', *Company*, February 2001.

[14] J. Rayner, 'We want to be alone'.

[15] 'The Debate', *The Observer*, 5 November 2000

> It's all about quickie passion and short-term flings. You meet, you make it, you lose interest, you move on to the next one. Very 21st century ... The TWR is a reversal of the traditional 'three dates, then sex' pattern, because with each date you grow further apart.[16]

Furthermore, singleness in its contemporary definition of 'not currently in a sexual relationship' does not preclude the possibility of sexual activity or searching for a partner. In fact, to be single is often to be in search of a partner.

Singleness in the original sense of virginity is becoming rarer. Despite the increase in the number of people classified as single or living alone, far fewer are celibate. The British Household Panel Survey carried out life-history research to discover how many women had ever been married or cohabited. It based its results on four age cohorts of women: those born in the 1900s, 1920s, 1940s and 1960s. It found that more women are now entering cohabiting partnerships (whether or not they actually marry) and at an earlier stage in life. While 17 per cent of women born in the 1920s had neither married nor cohabited by the age of thirty, for those born in the 1960s the figure was only 8 per cent.[17]

More women are having a greater number of sexual partners. A government survey in 1998 found that only 13 per cent of women (roughly a third of single women) had had no sexual partners in the previous year (76 per cent had one, 11 per cent had two or more). Only 5 per cent of women aged between sixteen and forty-four have never had a sexual partner, according to the 2001 National Survey of Sexual Attitudes and Lifestyles. The survey also found that two-thirds of women have had more than two sexual partners ever.[18] British Social Attitudes surveys have charted the relaxation in attitudes towards sexual behaviour: only 8 per cent of the population now think that premarital

[16] Kate le Vann, 'It only takes a fortnight', *Company*, January 2001.

[17] Central Statistical Office, *Social Focus on Women* (London: HMSO, 1995), 13.

[18] Sarah Boseley, 'More sex please – we're young, female, liberated and British', *The Guardian*, 30 November 2001.

sex is always wrong.[19] The age at which people are first having sex is decreasing. In the last ten years, the average age at which teenagers lose their virginity has fallen from seventeen to sixteen.[20]

Women's gender scripts (their ways of living as women in society) are changing. Women's behaviour in the second half of the twentieth century can (to some degree) be split into two categories, corresponding to their age. Women born before 1960 were regarded as future wives, housewives and mothers. This was particularly true in the 1950s, where the enduring image was of the perfect wife and mother who warmed her husband's slippers by the fire and greeted him with his newspaper when he returned from work. To be a woman was to function within the private sphere of the home. The man, meanwhile, was the breadwinner and the head of the household. Sex for women was largely a wifely duty. Single women were viewed as failures. Marriage and the nuclear family were upheld by the concept of romantic love, in which women were expected to wait for 'Mr Right', their 'Knight in Shining Armour', who would 'sweep them off their feet' and provide lifelong companionship and intimacy.

The sexual revolution of the 1960s brought changes, as women were encouraged to enjoy their sexual experiences. 'Free love' meant being sexually available and sexually active. Yet the convergence of the idea of women as sexually free and the 1950s housewife ideal led to a contradiction known as the sexual double standard. Women were expected to be sexually free for men, yet at the same time female sexual enjoyment was regarded as lewd or bad. Men were expected to 'sow their wild oats' and therefore find women who would enable them to do this, but women were expected to remain pure for their future husbands.

Women born after 1960 have witnessed an extension of the belief that women both want and need sexual experiences. Women's new sexual power is linked to their socio-economic

---

[19] Office for National Statistics, *Social Trends 30*, 41.
[20] S. Boseley, 'More Sex Please'.

independence from men. In the area of sex, some contemporary
women are becoming 'the New Men'. Whereas women used to
regard men romantically, now they view them as sources of
sexual pleasure. They are prepared to initiate sexual relationships rather than waiting for the men to do it. 'What do women
want from a man? Not too much, it seems – sex, the odd bit of
DIY. But increasingly they can do without cohabitation',
reported *The Observer*.[21] To be single and celibate is now
unusual. As Germaine Greer observed, 'Among the consequences of the loosening of sexual mores is that the single state is
now less respectable than it has ever been.'[22] Claire Evans, similarly, comments: 'Sex becoming the norm has placed the social
stigma that adultery and premarital sex once had onto celibacy.
Virginity has become a spectacle.'[23]

Without doubt, the increase in the number of single people
has resulted in their needs becoming better catered for within
society. Housing complexes geared to singles are being built,
complete with bars and gyms; the range of ready meals in super-
markets is expanding; books, films and television programmes
featuring single characters are becoming commonplace, and
singles' holidays and dating services proliferate. There are now
around seven hundred registered introduction agencies in the
UK. It is estimated that one in five single people, some two
million Britons, use dating services.[24]

Yet despite this, single people's socio-economic status remains
a significant issue. The married remain the beneficiaries of tax
concessions. A couple can share the cost of a one-bedroom flat a
single would have to purchase or rent alone. Singles are regularly
required to pay a single person supplement when holidaying in
hotels. Single women in particular tend to be poor. In her study

---

[21] F. Gibson, 'No Strings Attached'.
[22] Germaine Greer, *The Whole Woman* (London: Anchor, 2000), 312.
[23] Claire Evans, 'A Theological Response to the Issues of Singleness
within 18–35 year olds in the Western Church Today', Undergraduate
Thesis, London Bible College, 2001.
[24] Susan Elderkin, 'A Mission to Match', *Hotline*, Spring 2001.

of women without husbands, Joan Chandler notes that historically, 'lone women have always been disproportionately poor'.[25] In 1999, women's weekly earnings were only three-quarters of those of men.[26] The difference in earnings between single men and single women was less pronounced, with single women earning 86 per cent as much as single men.[27] Retirement can be bleak for the single woman. Her income during her working life is lower than the average man's, resulting in a smaller pension. Furthermore, she does not have a husband whose pension provision extends to her. Although married women may earn marginally less from employment than single women, their standard of living is higher because their husbands financially support them. Jennifer Kane Coplon's study of single older women in the workforce found that 'Unlike men and married women, single women over age 54 generally cannot look forward to retirement free of economic worry.'[28]

Loneliness is a significant problem for single people, although it is less so for women. A 1993 MORI poll demonstrated that loneliness was what single people admitted to disliking most about living alone. Journalist Nicci Gerrard notes that despite the sharp increase in methods of communication, loneliness is actually more widespread. Loneliness remains 'the last taboo'.[29] The question of the relative happiness of single and married people has long been argued over. What does appear to be true is that for women, loneliness is less of a problem than it is for men. In 1999 Richard Scase, author of the Britain Towards 2010 research project, found 'a growing segregation between the lives of single men and women'. He wrote:

[25] Joan Chandler, *Women without Husbands: An Exploration of the Margins of Marriage* (Basingstoke: Macmillan, 1991), 92.
[26] Office for National Statistics, *Social Trends 30*, 88.
[27] Office for National Statistics, *Social Trends 31*, 97.
[28] Jennifer Kane Coplon, *Single Older Women in the Workforce: By Necessity, or Choice?* (New York: Garland, 1997), xv.
[29] Nicci Gerrard, 'Will you be lonely this Christmas?', *The Observer*, 12 December 1999.

Single women in their thirties and forties have well-developed social networks and are involved in a wide range of activities. Men, on the other hand, appear to be sad, isolated, lonely cases. The hard truth seems to be that living alone is good for women, but bad for men.[30]

Pat Keith's study of elderly single people in the USA demonstrated that women had more contact with friends and relatives than men, and also reported a greater degree of happiness.[31] Never-married women were more content than widows. Single women have been seen to score higher on psychological well-being than both married women and single men.[32] Mental and physical health and longevity have been shown to be greater in those who have strong friendships and are involved in several different social networks.[33] Novelist William Sutcliffe suggests as a reason for increased singleness the reduction in traditional concepts of gender difference, which in turn has enabled non-sexual friendships between men and women to be formed more easily: 'Maybe we're staying single because we're getting more out of our friendships so the need for pair bonds reduces.'[34] However, a survey conducted by Mintel in 2001 found that, once single people reach their thirties, they are less likely to be happy than similarly aged couples. Over half the 'mid-life singles' (those over thirty-five) admitted to being sadder than five years ago, compared with just over a third of couples.[35]

Research has found that women's feelings about singleness are varied. Sandra Dalton produced a list of 13 different

---

[30] Julia Hartley-Brewer, 'Brave New Age Dawns for Single Women', *The Guardian*, 18 October 1999.

[31] Pat M. Keith, *The Unmarried in Later Life* (New York: Praeger, 1989).

[32] G. Greer, *The Whole Woman*, 326.

[33] Claire Ainsworth, 'In sickness and in health', *The Observer*, 5 November 2000.

[34] J. Rayner, 'We want to be alone'.

[35] Anne Campbell, 'Single and over 35? It's a sad, lonely life', *Metro*, 5 March 2001.

categories of meanings of singleness for the never-married women she questioned, noting that singleness has a 'multifaceted nature not only for different women, but also for individual women at different points in time'.[36] Karen Lewis and Sidney Moon's interview and questionnaire research revealed that 'single women have unresolved or unrecognized ambivalence about being single', an assertion which they expand as follows:

1 Single women are aware of both the advantages and the drawbacks of being single.
2 Single women are ambivalent about the reasons for their singleness.
3 Although content with being single, many women simultaneously experience feelings of loss and grief.[37]

Marcelle Clements' study of over a hundred single American women similarly showed that 'there exists a very wide range of judgments among single women about being single, plus a spectrum of contradictory emotions that any one woman has over a period of time'.[38]

Tuula Gordon's 1994 cross-cultural study of Britain, Finland and the USA, based upon interviews with 75 single women aged over thirty-five, examined single women's place in contemporary society. Gordon describes singleness as 'a result of a complex interaction between structural, cultural and biographical aspects. It is not likely to be a clearcut choice'. Like other researchers, she observes that 'Single women are a heterogeneous group ... Therefore, simple categorisations are not possible when discussing their experiences of being single.' Gordon examines the issue of gender difference and finds that single

---

[36] Sandra T. Dalton, 'Lived Experiences of Never-Married Women', *Issues in Mental Health Nursing* 13 (2) (1992), 69–80.

[37] Karen Gail Lewis and Sidney Moon, 'Always Single and Single Again Women: A Qualitative Study', *Journal of Marital and Family Therapy* 23 (2) (1997), 115–134.

[38] Marcelle Clements, *The Improvised Woman: Single Women Reinventing Single Life* (New York: W.W. Norton & Company, 1998), 17.

women are placed in an ambiguous and problematic position with regard to marriage, family and stereotypical femininity. Womanhood has traditionally been associated with wifehood and motherhood, yet single women are not, by definition, wives and mothers. This leads to the question of whether single women are 'proper' women. Historically, the answer given by many to this has been 'no', and single women have been treated as if they were somehow second-class, even a 'third sex'. Gordon remarks:

> Though single women today are in a different position from spinsters of the nineteenth century and old maids of the 1950s, marital status has not disappeared as a crucial category in establishing normality and deviation from it.

Many single women struggle with the experience of being on the margins of society. While the lifestyles of the married, or at least the partnered, are constantly reinforced by social interaction, cultural patterns and by the media, single women's lifestyles are more rarely legitimized. As a result, single people are more likely to have reflected on their singleness than married people have done on their marriedness. Consequently, single women have to work to 'negotiate their inside/outside spaces and engage in a learning process while doing so'. Gordon concludes with the observation that 'Tensions between separateness and connectedness, and between independence and intimacy, pose a tightrope for single women.'[39]

Work by Natalie Schwartzberg, Kathy Berliner and Demaris Jacob of the Clinical Project on Singlehood at The Family Institute of Westchester, USA, shows the problems faced by singles living in a society dominated by married people. In the foreword to their book, Betty Carter writes:

> Single people ... have been relegated to the margins of a society in which marriage not only is the norm but is presented as the only 'healthy' solution to the existential dilemmas of life. And the selling

---

[39] Tuula Gordon, *Single Women: On the Margins?* (Basingstoke: Macmillan, 1994), 63–4, 157, 126, 105, 198.

of marriage as the 'solution' continues in spite of all the facts and statistics that show it to be an institution experiencing deep troubles.[40]

Schwartzberg, Berliner and Jacob argue that single people need
to understand the way in which marriage has developed and is
still regarded as a social norm and requirement for passage into
adulthood. As therapists, they see a need to address the issues
faced by single people on three levels: the personal, the familial
and the societal. They encourage singles to revise their concept of
the human lifecycle. Rather than assume everyone must experience rites of passage, such as marriage and having children,
single people need to learn how to develop authentic and fulfilling lives within their single state.

The question of who remains single is linked to gender and
socio-economic status. Kathleen Kiernan's study of never-
married men and women found that single women 'are more
likely to have higher general ability scores, and to be highly educated and in high status occupations, while single men are more
likely to be members of the lowest social class or unemployed'.[41]
Because is it still common for men to marry women of a lower
educational level, the most highly educated women are likely to
have difficulty finding partners. The higher the educational level
of women, the more likely they are to remain childless.[42] The
prominence of economically successful single women is likely to
account for the media's particular concentration on the phenomenon of the single thirty-something woman.

The huge success of Helen Fielding's *Bridget Jones's Diary*
brought the situation of single women to the forefront of public

---

[40] Betty Carter, 'Foreword', in Natalie Schwartzberg, Kathy Berliner
and Demaris Jacob, *Single in a Married World: A Life Cycle Framework
for Working with the Unmarried Adult* (New York: W.W. Norton &
Company, 1995), ix.

[41] Kathleen E. Kiernan, 'Who Remains Celibate?', *Journal of Biosocial
Science* 20 (3) (1988), 253–263.

[42] Kathleen E. Kiernan and Éva Lelièvre, 'Great Britain' in Hans-Peter
Blossfeld (ed.), *The New Role of Women: Family Formation in Modern
Societies* (Oxford: Westview, 1995) 126–149,142.

consciousness. *Bridget Jones's Diary* tells the story of a weight-obsessed thirty-something woman for whom life is disordered and unhappy without a man. Bridget drifts through the year in pursuit of romance yet unable to attain it. While Bridget attempts to see singleness in a positive light and mocks her married friends, referring to them as 'Smug Marrieds', she nevertheless envies those who have partners. 'I will not sulk about having no boyfriend, but develop inner poise and authority and sense of self as woman of substance, complete without boyfriend, as best way to obtain boyfriend', she resolves at the beginning of the year.[43] At the end of the year, Bridget achieves her goal, finding love in the shape of Helen Fielding's Jane Austen-modelled Mark Darcy.

The Bridget Jones stereotype may by now be partially 'outmoded', as an *Observer* journalist suggested,[44] yet she has made an indelible mark on the landscape of British singledom. *Bridget Jones's Diary* tapped into the late 1990s *Zeitgeist* in which women agonized over their calorie consumption and their lack of romantic success. 'I am Bridget,' many a woman sighed with relief. Yet the 1990s Bridget Joneses found no practical solution to this female anxiety, other than finding a partner. Finding a partner, though portrayed as if it were as difficult as finding a four-leaf clover, is in fact easier for younger single women than it is for single men, for up to the age of forty-five, there are significantly more single men than there are women. The impression of the existence of a glut of single women created by the Bridget Jones phenomenon may be false. It is simply that there is a glut of highly educated single women. Personal ads in newspapers consistently contain a higher number of advertisements placed by men than by women. Bridget Jones authenticated and stimulated a kind of female neurosis in which women are seen (and see themselves) as needy and foolish, yet despite this continue fighting losing battles against age, imagined ugliness and the single state.

---

[43] Helen Fielding, *Bridget Jones's Diary* (London: Picador, 1997), 2.
[44] J. Rayner, 'We want to be alone'.

Another media image of single womanhood came in the form of Ally McBeal, thirty-something lawyer in the hit American television show of the same name. Ally is thin, attractive and successful, yet a failure in love. Like Bridget Jones, she is neurotic and obsessive about her lack of a partner. This sort of neurosis is prevalent among single women. In 2000 an NOP study for an online dating service found that twice as many women as men think they will never marry. The reason given was that these women 'refuse to settle for "Mr Making Do" rather than "Mr Right" '. *Times* journalist Catherine O'Brien, commenting on the new 'Bachelor Girls' typified by Ally McBeal, describes such women as 'self-obsessed', lacking in 'rationale' and unhealthily reliant on alcohol and comfort eating. She concludes 'Germaine Greer and Ann Widdecombe swear by BG status, but they are the exception. Inside most BGs is a BJ (Bridget Jones) who longs only to be married with two children and living in a big house in the country.'[45]

A report from the Family Policies Studies Centre revealed that in 2000, just under a quarter of children were living in single-parent households, the vast majority headed by a woman. Single mothers, though generally stereotyped as being teenagers living in council accommodation, are in fact as diverse as any other section of society. The National Child Development Study followed a thousand children born in Great Britain in one week in 1958 until the age of thirty-three. It found that 17 per cent of all women in the cohort had at some stage been lone mothers by the time they reached thirty-three. For the majority, lone parenthood was not permanent and a new partnership was subsequently formed. When they first became single parents, a quarter of the women were not living with a partner. Over 80 per cent of the lone mothers had at some stage lived with a partner.[46] These

---

[45] Catherine O'Brien, 'The Test – Bachelor Girls', *The Times,* July 19 2000.

[46] Joan Payne and Martin Range, *Lone Parents' Lives: An Analysis of Partnership, Fertility, Employment and Housing Histories of the 1958 British Birth Cohort,* Department of Social Security Research Report No.78 (London: The Stationery Office, 1998), 1, 23, 24.

figures suggest that single parenthood occurs largely as a result of relationship breakdown, rather than as a result of casual sexual encounters.

However, a few women have borne children after giving up on finding a suitable partner. In her research into this new family form in the United States, Naomi Miller noted that the majority of those termed 'Single Parents by Choice' are women. They tend to be successful professional women who have not found a partner with whom they want to have a child.[47] In the UK, newsreader Kirsty Lang described herself to *The Times* as a 'SMC – a Single Mother by Choice'. Lang comments: 'I tell my friends I failed to find a perfect man, so I grew my own.'[48]

Financially, lone parents are more likely to be badly off. Their incomes are, on average, well below half those of two-parent families with the same number of children.[49] A report from the Child Support Agency revealed that only 48 per cent of fathers regularly pay full child support, and 29 per cent pay nothing at all.[50]

In Britain, four in every ten marriages end in divorce. Predictions suggest that by 2010, seven in ten adults will have been married and divorced. The average age of divorce is rising: for men it is currently forty-one and for women it is thirty-eight.[51] There has also been a rapid rise in the number of long-standing marriages which break down. While women are more likely to initiate divorce proceedings (two in three divorces are granted to wives), men are more likely than women to take a new partner after divorce. For women, divorce tends to be harder to recover

[47] Naomi Miller, *Single Parents by Choice: A Growing Trend in Family Life* (New York: Plenum Press, 1992).

[48] Kirsty Lang, 'Bridget Jones – with child', *The Times,* 29 March 2000.

[49] Reuben Ford, Alan Marsh and Louise Finlayson, *What Happens to Lone Parents: A Cohort Study 1991–1995,* Department of Social Security Research Report No. 77 (London: The Stationery Office, 1998), 9.

[50] Amelia Hill, 'Divorce: he's richer, she's poorer', *The Guardian,* 22 October 2000.

[51] Francis Gibb, 'Divorce rates fall to lowest for 10 years', *The Times,* 6 December 2000.

from. *Times* journalist Mary Gould cited the new acronym 'Dacmos' (Divorced And Can't Move On) to refer to women who are left with the children after divorce. They find it difficult to meet a new partner, partly because the British population is made up of more divorced women than men, and find it hard to forgive their previous spouses.[52] Divorced women are also substantially worse off financially than divorced men. Research funded by the Economic and Social Research Council, which tracked ten thousand people over a decade, found that men's disposable income increases by 15 per cent after divorce, while women's falls by 28 per cent.[53]

Perhaps not surprisingly, given the media's focus on youth, widowhood has been neglected. Though the number of women who are widows is nearly double the number who are divorced, the situation of widows is rarely publicly discussed. As Helena Znaniecka Lopata's study of widowhood in the United States demonstrated, widows lack a distinct and permanent role within society. Many assumptions are made about them, yet widows are in fact a heterogeneous group. Znaniecka Lopata concludes:

> All in all, however, the image of widowhood that is emerging from current research is of a resilient widowed woman, able to work through her grief, cutting ties with the deceased, accepting life without him, modifying existing social relationships and roles and building new ones, and reconstructing the self into an independent, whole human being.[54]

Women are far more likely than men to be widowed. In 1997, while 72 per cent of men aged seventy to seventy-nine were married and only 17 per cent widowed, 42 per cent of women

---

[52] Mary Gould, 'Women on the verge of a brave new world', *The Times,* 18 November 2000.

[53] A. Hill, 'Divorce: he's richer, she's poorer'.

[54] Helena Znaniecka Lopata, *Current Widowhood: Myths and Realities* (London: Sage, 1996), 221–222.

were married and 47 per cent widowed. This is because men tend to be older than their wives, women live longer and widowers are more likely than widows to remarry. While men tend to end their lives cared for by their wives, elderly women are twice as likely as men to end up living in an institution. Half the women aged sixty-five and over live alone, compared to only a quarter of men.[55]

Singleness in the church

In 1998, the English Church Attendance survey found that evangelicals represented 2.8 per cent of the UK population, and around a third of the whole churchgoing population.[56] Approximately 60 per cent of evangelicals are female.[57] There are nearly half a million single evangelical Christians in the UK. According to these percentages, 334,000 women (0.7 per cent of the population), are single evangelical women. There are only 153,000 single evangelical men (0.3 per cent of the population) in comparison.

The most recent research, produced by the Evangelical Alliance in 1991, revealed that singles make up 35 per cent of evangelical adult church membership. This figure is slightly lower than the percentage of people in society who are not married, but slightly higher than the percentage of people in society who are not living with a partner. The study showed that 63 per cent of Christian singles had never married, 4 per cent were separated, 9 per cent were divorced and 24 per cent were widowed. In comparison with contemporary society, the church attracts a higher proportion of never-married people and widows, but a lower

---

[55] Office for National Statistics, *Social Focus on Older People* (London: The Stationery Office, 1999), 13, 19.
[56] Peter Brierley (ed.), *UK Christian Handbook: Religious Trends 2000/ 2001 No.2* (London: Christian Research, 1999), 12.3.
[57] Peter Brierley (ed.), *Prospects for the Nineties: Trends and Tables from the 1989 English Church Census* (London: MARC Europe, 1991), 24.

proportion of divorcees. The Evangelical Alliance survey noted a further category of singles termed 'church singles'. Church singles, who make up 9 per cent of church members, are those whose spouses do not attend church. They are more likely to be female.

There are more single women than men in church within all age groups. Overall, 68 per cent of single adult members of evangelical churches are women, and only 32 per cent are men. Within the younger age groups, this ratio is less pronounced: 56 per cent of singles under thirty are female. As singles get older, the imbalance becomes greater. In the forty-five to fifty-nine age band, there are three times more women than men, and for the over-sixties, women outnumber their male counterparts by six to one.[58]

The gender dimension of these figures gives cause for concern, for they reveal a lack of men in church where there is no similar lack in society. While single women remain church members whether or not they marry, it would appear that some single men are giving up on church, and the vast majority are failing to be attracted to Christianity in the first place. The lack of men in church has been explained by a number of different theories. Some have hypothesized that women's increased religiosity is due to their greater responsibility as primary childrearers in teaching their children moral values. This, however, does not explain single women's religiosity. Other sociologists claim that religion is more suited to those with a 'feminine' personality orientation, the majority of whom will be women. Another personality theory states that women feel more guilt than men and are more submissive, and that since religion is dependent on its adherents submitting to God for forgiveness of guilt or sin, women are more likely to convert.[59] Male children of churchgoing parents are also more

---

[58] Steve Chilcraft *One of Us: Single People as Part of the Church* (Milton Keynes: Nelson Word, 1993), 73–4

[59] For an overview of theories of religious differences between men and women, see William K. Kay and Leslie J. Francis, *Drift from the Churches: Attitude toward Christianity During Childhood and Adolescence* (Cardiff: University of Wales Press, 1996), 10–16.

likely to drop out of church. This is because girls tend to be brought up to be more conformist than boys.[60]

There are several other possible reasons for the lack of men in evangelical churches. It may be the case that women are more active in evangelizing same-sex friends than their male counterparts. Church-based evangelistic projects are more likely to be directed at women than at men, with mother and toddler clubs a common initiative laid on by churches. It is also likely that there is a connection between the large proportion of unmarried Christian women and the socio-economic status of churchgoers. As already noted, single women in UK society are generally better educated than single men. In addition to this, church membership tends to be heavily weighted towards the middle classes and to lack members from the lowest socio-economic groups.[61] This leads to the conclusion that the high proportion of unmarried Christian women and low proportion of single Christian men is indicative of the church's largely middle-class constituency.

Single Christians have been found to be less active in leadership within local churches. The Evangelical Alliance survey found that singles filled only a quarter of all leadership positions, including house group leading and PCC roles. It further discovered that only 50 per cent of churches used singles to lead house groups. The most common role for singles was leadership of youth work or children's work. Nearly three-quarters of churches had single people involved in leading children's work, the majority of whom were single women. In his research on power and abuse in the contemporary church, Paul Beasley-Murray found that 96 per cent of the ministers in his sample were married. He comments:

---

[60] Hart M. Nelsen, 'Religious Conformity in an Age of Disbelief: Contextual Effects of Time, Denomination, and Family Processes upon Church Decline and Apostasy', *American Sociological Review* 46 (1981), 632–640.
[61] Robin Gamble, *The Irrelevant Church* (Eastbourne: Monarch, 1991), 118.

As far as single clergy are concerned, in the more evangelical
churches, if not generally, there tends to be a bias against the unmarried ... When seeking a minister, most churches want a married man
with 2.4 children ... What amounts to a 'dearth' of single ministers
means that ministry – and therefore its emphases – is quite unrepre-
sentative of Britain as a whole, where out of some 46 million nearly
17 million – over one third (36%) – are single.[62]

Research into issues facing single evangelical Christians in the
eighteen to thirty-five age group conducted by Claire Evans at
London Bible College unveiled attitudes of church leaders and
their single members. Out of a sample of thirty single men and
thirty single women, seven out of ten had never heard a sermon
on singleness. Consequently, few singles had much knowledge of
what the Bible says about singleness. When asked 'do you think
Christians view singleness as being equal or inferior to marriage?' three-quarters of the men and all but one of the women
said they felt that Christians view singleness as inferior to marriage. One man commented, 'I feel married people are more
valued in ministry', noting his church's preference for married
house group leaders. It is therefore hardly surprising that when
asked to list positive and negative aspects of singleness, far more
negatives were listed.

While few had used a dating service, a third of the sample of
sixty said they would consider searching for a partner through a
dating agency. The majority of these were men. Men were also
more likely than women to date non-Christians: over a half of
the men and just over a quarter of the women admitted to having
dated someone who was not a Christian. Of these, almost half
said they would still be happy to date a non-believer. Asked what
attracted them most to a member of the other sex, 'good looks'
and 'spirituality' gained the most marks, 'good looks' being cited
as the most important factor. Women were marginally less influenced by looks and ranked spirituality and physical appearance

---

[62] Paul Beasley-Murray, *Power for God's Sake: Power and Abuse in the
Local Church* (Carlisle: Paternoster, 1998), 27.

as equally important. While all said they were leading a sexually
celibate lifestyle, two-thirds of men and half the women admitted to finding it a struggle. The younger the women, the more
they struggled with living a celibate lifestyle. Claire Evans attributes this to an increasing societal pressure to be sexually active.[63]

Surveys conducted by the Universities and Colleges Christian
Fellowship into sex and relationship issues faced by Christian
students revealed that the majority had never heard any Christian teaching on relationships or sex-related matters. Asked
what their greatest personal struggle in this area is, men's top five
struggles were 1) Masturbation, 2) Images on film, videos and
magazines, 3) The way women dress, 4) Memories of the past
and 5) Not having a girlfriend. For women, the principal struggles were 1) Fear of singleness 2) Not having a boyfriend, 3)
Memories of the past, 4) Pressure from boyfriend and 5) Masturbation.[64] It is significant that women's top two struggles were
related to not wanting to be single.

Just as singleness in contemporary society now seldom means
celibacy, so Christian singleness in its biblical sense of a gift used
for service to God and others, appears to be becoming rarer.
Christian organizations, such as holiday companies, dating
agencies, social clubs, Christian balls, and dance classes, have
sprung up to cater for the perceived needs of singles to find partners. Serial dating seems to be becoming more common amongst
Christians. Advertisements placed by Christians seeking partners can regularly be found in the personal columns of mainstream newspapers. The vast majority of single Christians want
to marry. In 1997, the Church Pastoral Aid Society produced a
booklet on singleness, in which it stated that 'In surveys, up to
ninety per cent of single people say they would prefer to be
married.'[65] Though Christians may tacitly agree that singleness is
a gift, it is the gift almost no one wants.

[63] C. Evans, 'A Theological Response to the Issues of Singleness'.
[64] Nigel D. Pollock, *The Relationships Revolution* (Leicester: Inter-
Varsity Press, 1998), 26–7.
[65] Steve Chilcraft, Sheena Gillies and Rory Keegan, *Single Issues: A
Whole-Church approach to Singleness* (Warwick: CPAS, 1997), 8.

2

Church

The purpose of this study is twofold. Its focus is both single Christian women and the church they inhabit. While this research is concerned with the issues which face single Christian women, the number and strength of the ninety or so single women's views also allow the church itself to be examined and critiqued. While the church has been analysed from the perspective of church leaders and academics, it is rare for the voices of church members to be heard so clearly. It is also rare for both single people and women to be involved in the study of church life. This study of single evangelical women is the first of its type to be undertaken in the UK.

The majority of the women involved in this research had never married. This is partly due to the fact that the 1998 research looked only at never-married women. It is also because the snowball email method of data collection used in 2001 yielded responses from women who were more conversant with email, and were therefore younger. This means that the age range of the women was not representative of single evangelical women as a whole. The average age of the women involved in this research was thirty-three. The majority of these women were under forty, and so more likely to be never-married than widowed or divorced. In comparison with the Evangelical Alliance's far larger sample, in which 33 per cent of single women were under thirty and 42 per cent under forty-five, 58 per cent of women in the sample for this book were under thirty and 81 per cent under forty-five. The Evangelical Alliance research found that 63 per cent of singles (men and women) were never-married, 4 per cent were separated, 9 per cent were divorced and 24 per cent were widowed.[1] As for the sample for this book, 89 per cent were never-married, 1 per cent were separated, 7 per cent were divorced and only 3 per cent were widowed. Because of the large proportion of never-married women, these chapters sideline the issues faced by divorced and widowed women. The imbalance in age also means that issues faced by single women over forty-five are given less space. Both of these facts are regrettable.

No questions were asked in the questionnaire about occupation or socio-economic status. Anonymity was assured at the outset of the process. All names of women in this book are pseudonyms but ages have not been altered. Names of denominations or churches given in the women's responses have been obscured, as have all names of Christian organizations.

Defining singleness

Rather than defining singleness simply as being unmarried, almost all of the women defined singleness as not being in an exclusive 'going out' relationship with someone of the opposite sex. Singleness encompasses those who are never-married, divorced, separated and widowed. This definition is similar to that of contemporary society. Some saw it as 'being on one's own' or, in relation to one's living environment, 'living alone'. Others described it as a situation in which one is not accountable to anyone else. A few women defined singleness in positive terms:

> *Singleness is that happy state where one is self-reliant and independent.*
>
> Fiona, 32

---

[1] S. Chilcraft, *One of Us*, 71,73.

Yvonne (31) wrote:

> *Shame it's defined by 'not havings', rather than 'havings'. Hmm – try this – 'Having God as the only exclusive relationship in my life.'*

Others used negative terms:

> *Singleness is waiting not to be.*
>
> Sophie, 31

Some felt that their definition of singleness did not match that of their churches:

> *I would define singleness as not married or in a long-term relationship – including people who are divorced, separated and widowed. However, I think most people in evangelical churches tend not to recognize or legitimize even long-term relationships – only marriage is good enough.*
>
> Alice, 29

Harriet (30) commented:

> *Those who are in a sexual relationship but not 'legally' married I wouldn't define as 'single' – but that's because of my views on what constitutes 'marriage' in Christian terms! I think there are more people in this situation in the church than many realize!*

The main issues facing single Christian women

In response to the question: 'What are the main issues facing single Christian women?' six main response categories emerged. The most commonly cited issue was the church's attitude towards single women. This was closely followed by issues to do with men, sex and dating. Third came emotional issues associated with feelings about being single and facing the future. Next came questions of loneliness and social need, which was cited with the same frequency as the fifth category, roles and ministry within the church. The final category was concerned with the practicalities of living and working within contemporary society.

This chapter and the next each address three of these issues. This chapter focuses particularly on the church. It considers the church's attitude to single women, loneliness and the need for social provision, and single women's roles and ministry within the church. Chapter 3 addresses men, sex and dating, emotional issues around singleness, and living in contemporary society.

The church's attitude to single women

The church: Christ's body; God's people; the household or family of God; a community of believers in which each loves and is loved, serves and is served; the place where one is valued regardless of age, ethnicity, abilities or disabilities, economic, gender or marital status. This is the ideal, yet single women's experiences of church tend to fall short of this.

By far the most common response to the question: 'What are the main issues facing single Christian women?' brought up the question of identity within the church community. One third of the women noted that single women need a sense of belonging, identity and value as single people. They want an awareness of their self-worth, status and wholeness which is not dependent upon whether they marry. Dealing with other people's negative attitudes to their singleness is sometimes a major hurdle in their search for Christian identity, as is 'widespread Christian assumptions on Christians naturally desiring to be married and have children' (Mandy, 34). 'Pressure to get married and "conform" to what's expected … is not always a verbalized pressure, but it is always there,' remarked Leila (25). Some single women need to shed a 'negative self-image', which has come about from the perception of being 'left on the shelf' (Bethan, 24). As Jo (23) explained, 'In order to have a fulfilled place in the church they haven't to feel that they never quite achieve it unless they're married, because that would be continually working against them.' They need 'a sense of belonging' (Susan, 44), 'affirmation and approval' (Lisa, 31), to be 'accepted for who they are in God' (Maggie, 30), to 'find [their] identity in Christ and not in the usual female roles, such as wife and mother' (Denise, 23). They need to stop believing 'the fallacy that we are not a complete woman if we are not married' (Clare, 29). They want to be 'taken seriously' (Imogen, 23) and 'valued' (Sue, 41) 'not just for their babysitting potential' (Moira, 57, Sylvia, 72). Paula (28) believed valuing a single woman requires that she is not categorized as 'just one of many "single women"'. A few women were adamant that they did not wish to be categorized as having particular needs, but simply treated as individuals.

Part of this search for identity is connected to their need to discover how to fit into the family-oriented churches of which many of them are members. When churches 'promote everything family' (Sian, 41), single women tend to feel excluded. Esther (24) commented that 'there's a great deal of pressure to conform' in family-oriented church environments. Some felt that it was easier for women with children to integrate into a church community. Several sensed that they were viewed as a 'threat' by married people, though none elaborated on what they meant by this. Some wondered how single women were viewed in relation to male 'headship': Lisa (31) noted that single women face the question of 'how they function without the leadership and "covering" of a husband'.

Loneliness and social life

Loneliness and the need for a social life was cited as the fourth most prominent issue for single Christian women. Single women often experience isolation and loneliness within church environments. This is largely due to there being few other singles (or few in their particular age group) in their local church. City churches tend to contain a higher proportion of single people; village churches contain very few. Loneliness tends to be felt more acutely in churches which put a strong emphasis on the needs of nuclear families.

In response to the question: 'How easy is it for single women to be involved in the social life of a church?' roughly half of the women said it was relatively or very easy. Two out of ten said it depended on a number of factors, such as age, size of church, the attitude of the woman and the attitude of married people towards her. Three out of ten said it was relatively or very difficult for single women to be involved. It was noticeable that those who said it was easy tended to be under thirty-five, while those who said it was difficult tended to be over thirty-five. This demonstrates that as women age, having a social life becomes increasingly difficult. The fact that most women in the sample were younger than the average single woman suggests that, had the sample been more representative, a greater proportion would have stressed single women's lack of access to social interaction with other church members.

Women who were fulfilled in their social lives cited their youth, the large proportion of single people in their churches, and participation in special interest groups (student, twenties and thirties, single women's). A number said that other single women, particularly of their own particular status group (never-married, divorced or widowed) provided friendship and solidarity. Becky (20) noted:

> The singles can almost be more involved because they do not have a family to spend time with. Married couples with children are less able to go to the evening meetings because of their children.

A few commented that married couples had provided hospitality for them. Several spoke of being used as babysitters. While one woman said this had helped her to get to know a family, most others did not like being asked to babysit. Jennifer (45) related a 'very real and painful experience':

> I discovered that my house group had all been out to celebrate a wedding anniversary whilst I had willingly babysat. I had thought they'd just gone out for a meal with friends and the lack of honesty really wounded me.

Bridget (43) was similarly negative:

> *My biggest gripe was being asked to babysit by people who seemed to expect that I had a duty to serve in this way. If I was ever invited round for a meal, it was with the children. This gave me a sense that you only really became an adult when you are married, whatever your age.*

A significant number of women commented on their feeling that church social events were geared to couples and families. Sandra (50) felt disadvantaged by a distinctive church social culture in which single women could not easily fit:

> *We do not fit the middle-class Christian pattern of being married with a family. There are some welcome exceptions but I guess the norm is for supper parties to be even numbers.*

Some women cited as an issue facing single women the need for increased social opportunities. They wanted to have more openings for the formation of close friendships, not only with other single women, but also platonic friendships with single men. Anna (26) pointed out that single women face the problem of 'how to get to know male friends without them always thinking you have an ulterior motive'. Alice (29) felt similarly:

> *It's an irritation for single women that if you are seen with a male friend, automatic assumptions are made … 'cos people are so keen to see you paired off.*

Annabel (28) reflected:

> *In my experience, single Christian men tend to be very wary of spending much time with single Christian women, even in groups, which makes it hard to build friendships. I'd love to feel like some of the single men at my church saw me as a sister in Christ (1 Timothy 5:2), rather than as a potential stumbling-block.*

Yvonne (31) agreed that other Christians' perceptions of single people's 'intimate friendships' was a problem, in that a single woman who has a close male friend may be viewed as 'loose', and a single woman who has a close female friend may be seen as 'lesbian'.

Roles and ministry in the church

Roles and ministry within the church was the fifth most important issue for the women in the sample. Single women want opportunities to serve within their churches. Yet the ambiguities connected to Christians' perceptions of their status may render their access to ministry opportunities problematic. A quarter of women felt that single women's roles in church was a major issue for them. Knowing they are valued, the key issue facing single women, often comes about through being given opportunities to serve the church. Similarly, not being valued shows itself through lack of access to roles of service. This comment made by Nadia (27), whose church gives greater ministry opportunities to married women, sums this up:

> *People should treat single women as if the singleness does not mean that you're incomplete. You're complete and whole as a single woman, just as a married woman is. You're equally usable and you have equal ability to speak into people's lives ... In terms of your gifting and talents and in terms of service, singleness or marriage is not an issue ... I think the church needs to give room for single women to be involved in leadership.*

Some women felt, as Tamsin (28) did, that:

> *For some, the opportunities they have to serve the church are limited, especially within leadership. Sometimes they are only given a few alternatives, and mainly have to be under a man or a married woman.*

Harriet (30) believes that single women face 'battles ... within the church in trying to use [our] "gifts" to serve the church when this entails positions of responsibility or leadership which are "male" dominated.' Jean (53) felt that both married and single women's ministry is marginalized in the church situation:

> *Can you be taken seriously? Do you have an opportunity to enter-*
> *tain desires and thoughts of a vocation within the church, and can*
> *one be accepted in leadership positions without patronization and*
> *tokenism?*

Several felt the lack of positive role models of single women in ministry. Others commented that single women risk 'being given all the odd jobs in church "because you haven't got any other commitments"' (Yvonne, 31). Yvonne saw this as a problem for the way women value themselves, noting that single women need to learn how to say no and give themselves time off.

Amy (28) is involved in cross-cultural ministry to Middle Eastern women, who are all married with children, and feels her single status makes this harder, as she shares with them few 'common life experiences'. Annabel (28) felt her gender made her marital status an issue when considering paid Christian employment:

> *I'm doing 'part-time' Christian work, and considering the possibili-*
> *ties for full-time work in the future. Making any sort of long-term*
> *decisions is complicated by the fact that what I'm going to be doing*
> *in five or ten years' time depends entirely on whether I'm still single*
> *or married by then. I know that there's an element of uncertainty for*
> *men, too, but in most cases their ministry can continue largely*
> *unchanged alongside the arrival of a wife and even kids, in a way*
> *that a woman's can't.*

The question: 'What opportunities for leading and serving are available to single women within the evangelical churches you've been part of? Are single women discriminated against in this? If so, in what ways?' sought to discover how well single women were involved in ministry within the church.

It is important to note that women noted or denied discrimination according to their individual theological views about women's roles. Those who believe female church leadership is biblically justifiable will see discrimination where women do not have access to such leadership roles, yet for those who do not believe in female leadership, lack of access to leadership roles is not viewed as discrimination. Nikki's (20) answer exemplifies this view:

> *There are not many single women around in my church, but opportunities in various things (crèche, Sunday Club, Mothers Group, Alpha, home groups, worship etc.), certainly no discrimination. Women don't teach ... and I suppose women (married or single) don't ever lead main services either. Not sure if that is church policy and, if so, why ...*

Two-fifths of women said they did not think single women were discriminated against. The same proportion believed they were discriminated against and listed examples of this. The rest did not commit to an answer either way.

Single women take on a wide variety of serving and leading roles within their churches. Altogether, the women listed fifty different activities in which single women are involved. Women take on leadership roles as deacons, youth leaders, and even, very occasionally, as elders or pastors. They lead church services, music groups, teach Bible study groups and sometimes preach sermons. They read the Bible in services, lead prayer groups, give out communion, and help with prayer ministry and Alpha courses. They run the crèche and the children's work, head up social action work, cook and serve coffee. They are on the PCC, run arts events and speak at school and university Christian Unions. They oversee house groups, usher and help on homeless projects. Of all the roles cited, the most frequent were (in this order) children's work, music group, house group leading, preaching and youth work.

Rather than being discriminated against, a few women felt that single women had greater opportunities for ministry than married women. 'Single women are certainly not discriminated against,' said Vicky (28), adding that instead, they are 'almost more presumed upon'. Harriet (30) agreed: 'It is the married women who are discriminated against by the assumptions that they can no longer be involved in anything without their husband!' Carolyn (23) felt that single women were more able to serve within the church because they have 'control over their own time'. Amanda's (29) answer shows that giving single women more to do is not always a good thing: 'If anything, they may be exploited and there may be an assumption that they will do anything and everything because they showed willing at the start.' In Briony's (23) church, single women are very active:

> *Single women are seen as very useful for things like crèche and other roles within the church, which it would be thought difficult to ask someone with 'responsibilities' to other halves to do. This means most of the jobs in the church fall to single people, women mainly, as there are so few men.*

Alice (29) felt that women's singleness could be both a disadvantage and an advantage in ministry:

> *I know that some women in evangelical churches feel that they are discriminated against … However, in the majority of cases, I think the problems affect all women, not just single women. However, it might seem more obvious to a single woman, as she has more time for ministry, and wants to get more involved (rather than being caught up with children etc.) and might become more aware of the general discrimination facing women in the church – such as the obsession with not having women in leadership positions, etc.*

> *However, at least single women aren't subjected to the absurd notion of male leadership in marriage – hurrah! That's a definite advantage to being single. You are your own woman, instead of, for example, facing the 'dilemma' of how a female in some kind of leadership can minister in a church which includes her husband, who is (of course) in leadership over her. I kid you not! Hurrah for being single!*

Despite the fact that these half-dozen women felt that single women received greater opportunity for ministry than married women, twice that number felt that married women were given more of a role. Sophie (31) believes this is because the church leadership 'glorifies marriage'. Andrea (28) suggested that the reason for single women's lack of involvement in ministry is that 'they are not thought of as having the same full life experience as others'. Sue (41) and Angela (39) had both experienced churches where, though women's leadership was allowed, only married women operated as leaders. Moira (57) commented:

> I believe that with a husband in tow I would be more acceptable to the church in terms of giving support and ministry to others. I feel that I am perceived as being incomplete without a man, or certainly not as useful.

Frances (25) expressed her frustration at the lack of leadership opportunities available to single women in her denomination:

> Women take the more submissive role and don't become leaders, which makes me angry. Their role is just as strong as the man's in carrying the church, yet they must be 'behind' the man, which is strange. As a woman wanting, perhaps, to take on responsibilities within the church later, I know that I will not be trained up to lead, which, I believe, is where my strengths lie. The fact that this hasn't really been talked about and the women just accept it makes me feel the need to learn more ... You have to find a husband to help in the leading. Otherwise, I believe singleness does not stop opportunities.

Carrie (25) felt similarly that there was a lack of leadership opportunities for single women:

> Churches tend to go on the view that if they don't have a family, then they can't lead a group of people. I have never come across a single leader as an elder in any church. More trust seems to be given to married couples to lead small groups etc.

The women differed vastly as to their theological beliefs about how prominent a place women should have in the church. Some believed no roles should be differentiated by gender. A few believed in a principle of male leadership that extended beyond eldership to other aspects of church life. Imogen (23) said:

> *[Single women are involved] in homeless projects, teaching Sunday school, leading Alpha: their roles are mainly equal, except young men can take the collection and serve communion. I don't mind this. I think it's good for men to be assertive and leaders and to be encouraged to take initiative. The secular world does not teach this. We all contribute equally in Bible studies. I think women should learn to be responsive to men's initiative as I think this is the biblical perspective and opposite to the post-modern feminist world.*

Kitty (21) described the practice of the most conservative evangelical churches:

> *In strict evangelical churches, I have to admit that I see the treatment of women as a form of discrimination. Women are not permitted to lead mixed groups, teach in church, or even read the Bible or pray in some extreme cases. Where this is the case, women are largely consigned to roles they are not universally suited to – for example, children's work, or the pastoral care of other women. However, such churches would obviously argue that their position is biblically sound (which, again, I would question). Married women have more opportunities – especially in partnership with their husbands – since they can be involved in counselling of couples and other broader pastoral activities.*
>
> *In less narrow environments, single women can take part in worship-leading, small-group leading, teaching, reading, public prayer and even overall leadership in some cases. Discrimination against women is directly proportional to the extent that the Bible is interpreted literally in evangelical churches.*

The churches that were ideologically committed to restricting women's prominence varied in the roles women were forbidden from taking on. Some did not allow women to preach sermons, be elders or lead services. Others forbade women from giving communion, leading prayers, reading the Bible in a service or leading mixed-sex groups. Vanessa (35), who is involved with leading the music, said her previous church would not allow women this role:

> *They had four male worship leaders and the minister said it was very specific that they didn't have female worship leaders because they wanted a predominantly male front in order to help attract the men into the church.*

Several women commented that single women tended to be given predominantly 'serving roles'. Bethan (24) commented: 'The majority do children's church, visiting the elderly, the worship group and that is about it. It would be good to see some more men taking some of these roles.' Tamsin (28) said: 'Within some churches that I have come across, single women are considered 'weak' and can often be boxed into a stereotype – they can serve in the Sunday school or help out with catering etc.'

A good number of women commented that ideology and reality did not match up. Bridget (43) said that her denomination's ideological views about women's equal entitlement to leadership roles was not worked out in practice: 'There is an acknowledgement that women generally can lead and definitely serve but reality trails miserably behind this recognition.' Lorna (51), who had been given 'a lot of opportunities for ministry', felt that she had perhaps been unusually fortunate: 'I have on several occasions had comments like, "We don't normally ask (or allow) women to do this, but we don't mind when it is you". ' Annette (31) saw a need to more effectively utilize women's gift of singleness:

> *If there is discrimination in the church, I think that it's fairly unintentional, or not necessarily well thought out. It's more that people*

don't seem to know quite what to do with single women; we don't
exactly fit into any particular category ... and, like the majority of
single women I know seem to dream that one day they'll be married
... I think that the church might have adopted a similar attitude that
someday they will get married, so it isn't really an issue to be
addressed how to encourage, support and teach them. But we do
seem to settle for a lowest common denominator of how single
women can serve/be taught in the church. We don't really do much to
discover why God has kept them single for himself and how we can
use that gift for the blessing of the wider church. I would LOVE to
see more of these women explore their gifts so that they can be used
to benefit the church!

Positive and negative experiences of being a single woman in the church

In response to the question: 'Has your experience of being single
in evangelical churches been positive or negative?' two-fifths of
women said it had been predominantly or entirely positive; two-
fifths said it had been a mixture of both, and one-fifth said it had
been predominantly or entirely negative. Those whose experiences had been predominantly positive tended to be slightly
younger than those whose experiences had been predominantly
negative, which indicates that single women fare worse the older
they become. Asked to list the aspects which had contributed to
these positive or negative experiences, although more women
had said their church experience had been positive than negative,
women listed a greater number of negative aspects than they did
positive ones. A common response was: 'Mostly positive, but ...'
followed by a list of negatives.

Positive aspects of single women's church experience
The two most frequently cited aspects of church life which the
women found beneficial were the opportunities to form friendships with other singles and the opportunities for them to be
involved in ministry within the church. After these, most important was support and love received from other church members

Positive aspect of church experience	Number of women citing this
Good opportunities to have a good social life and form close friendships with other single Christians	19
Good opportunities to be involved in ministry within the church	16
Supported and loved by the church	12
Treated as an individual/not perceived as strange because single	11
Able to grow in own relationship with God	3
Good single female role models	3
Received helpful teaching on gender/singleness issues	2
Men who affirm single women	1
Services called 'all age' rather than 'family'	1
Church less preoccupied with singleness/marriage issues than society is	1
Able to do more outside the church	1
Made fuss of by other people's children on Mothering Sunday	1
Live in a church community house	1

and, linked to this, an acceptance of them as gifted individuals, rather than as peculiar because they were not married.

Opportunity to form close friendships with other single Christians

For most women who listed this as a positive aspect of church life, friendships with other single women were of paramount importance. For younger women this was easier, as there tend to be more single women in their twenties and thirties than in their forties and above.

Because I am young ... most people are single and I have lots of committed friendships at church and people to do things with and to care for me.

Becky, 20

I have generally been in churches where there have been a large number of young people, including single people, so there has been a definite culture of single people socializing in groups. This has been predominantly positive, although I can see how difficult it would be being a single woman in a church of young families.

Anna, 26

I have a rich source of friends who are all professional women now in their late thirties, early forties.

Bridget, 43

I have always been in a church where there are a good proportion of single people around and so it hasn't felt at all as if I am the only one. Some good groups have run for people in their twenties and thirties – what has been great about these groups is that they have been a mix of singles and marrieds, with both states treated the same.

Clare, 29

Involvement in ministry

I have constantly been affirmed, encouraged and released to be who God has made me to be and to fulfil the purposes he has for me!

Lisa, 31

I have been able to give a lot of my time to my church, and I've been able to serve according to my spiritual gifting (i.e. teaching and leading).

Hannah, 28

I have been given positions of responsibility in the church leadership in order to encourage the use of my gifts and what I enjoy doing to 'build up' the church. My church is probably unusual in that we have women preachers (but no ordained women on the staff).

Harriet, 30

Annette (31) described how, having moved from a church in which single women had little opportunity to be involved, she joined a church which allowed her to use her gifts:

> *As soon as I arrived in [...] I got hooked into a good evangelical church. The even more astounding thing was that they just desperately needed people to help out with anything ... so I found myself from the very beginning helping out teaching students in Bible studies and serving in the kitchen before our Christianity Explained groups. The most exciting thing for me was the fact that I had somewhere to serve God. And that I was needed and could be used in the body of Christ.*

Love and support received from church members

> *The church I go to is a big city church, which acts as a large family; there are lots of opportunities to get involved, and a good home group structure ... There is a good mentoring system, which ensures that maturity, whether a single person or not, is encouraged, i.e. the issue of singleness probably would not be ignored within a mentoring relationship but given encouragement so that it can be lived to its fullness.*
>
> Paula, 28

Some of the women spoke of being supported by the church through difficult times. Hilary's husband died at an early age from cancer:

> *The church family were as devastated as I was by my husband's death. We supported one another in our pain. Friends visited my husband, reading to him, praying with him, sharing in the last day, and caring for me in practical as well as prayerful ways. It had nothing to do with the label 'evangelical'; it was love in Christ. The church provided the meal for 300 people after the Thanksgiving Service. I have since always had people to share with, have meals with, do practical jobs for me.*
>
> Hilary, 55

Beryl's fiancé, a leader in her church, abruptly and without explanation called off their engagement:

> *The church and I have never got to the bottom of why he did it. But the church were most supportive, with prayer and just listening when I needed it.*

Beryl, 64

Acceptance of them as gifted individuals

> *I feel part of a 'family', so everyone knows me and I feel welcome.*

Emily, 20

> *I'm treated as a daughter and a sister by all.*

Imogen, 23

> *The majority of time I'm encouraged simply to live as a Christian – the fact that I'm single/a woman is not an issue.*

Tessa, 26

> *Being single has never been an issue. I have always been treated just like everyone else ... which is great, as obviously I am just like everyone else!*

Fiona, 32

Negative aspects of single women's church experience

Singleness is viewed by other Christians as inferior to marriage

In response to the question of whether church experiences had been negative or positive, over a third of the women said they felt their singleness was viewed as inferior to marriage. When answers to the rest of the questions were added to this, the total proportion of women who felt their singleness was viewed by their churches in a negative way came to around three-fifths.

Some women felt the church was unsure as to how to 'classify' them. 'I have found it difficult to "fit" as a single person in the church, as my particular church is very family-oriented', wrote

Negative aspect of church experience	Number of women citing this
Other Christians view singleness as inferior to marriage/pressure singles to marry	30
Isolation felt in company of Christian couples and families	17
Lack of ministry opportunities within the church	14
Church's unhelpful attitudes to dating	6
Personal desire for marriage/children	5
Lack of discussion/acknowledgement of issues related to singleness	5
Single women lack a 'voice' in the church	3
Single women are treated as children rather than adults	3
Church assumes single women will take on administrative roles	2
Few single female role models	2
Lack of support	1
Overprotective church leader	1
Other single people desperate to marry	1

Molly (26). Alison (20) agreed: 'At times I felt my status didn't fit into the general schema.' Yvonne (31) felt 'that one either has to fit into the gym-three-times-a-week-professional-woman or the trendy-housechurch-women-make-the-coffee-and-the-babies mould.' Sian (41), divorced after being left by her husband, wrote:

> *I still feel like a bit of an outcast at times. I went to a church training day and someone asked me about my marital status – when I said I was divorced it was assumed that I had found my faith after separation.*

Helen's (44) comment summed up many others:

> On the whole they don't understand that women can be single by choice and feel they must 'matchmake'. Churches push the ideals of family life and give the impression that you must have something wrong with you if you are still single.

Belinda (26) complained:

> The impression I strongly received was that being single was an option only second to marriage and that if you were single, you were really only waiting around to be married, as if there was nothing better to do in life(!) ... Singleness is viewed as a state in which people are pitied and it's assumed that I'm always lonely because I'm single. Genesis 2:18 ('It is not good that the man should be alone') was often cited as further evidence to support the idea of marriage being the preferred option.

Emily (20) felt that 'it seems very Christian to get married, with my friends anyway'. She added: 'Possibly Christians get married younger, for sex.' Alice (29), who is in a long-term relationship, said she felt pressured to marry her boyfriend:

> I have, for the last four years, been asked EVERY DAY and several times on Sundays when I'm getting married. To start with, this didn't bother me, but it's got to the point where it's driving me spare, and putting me off the idea of marriage altogether! Or making me wonder what my motivation would be to get married – for genuine reasons, or just to relieve the pressure from everyone else. Almost from the moment you start dating someone, the questions start – which I think is pretty unwise, considering Christians take marriage more seriously, and it's harder to get out of (!) – you'd think that you'd be counselled to be a lot more cautious and discerning before you signed your life away!

'Matchmaking tendencies' of other Christians were roundly denounced. Sarah (25) reflected:

There are a couple in my church who are avidly praying that I find my husband soon, and I get a bit fed up of the 'nudge nudge wink wink' attitude if a new bloke turns up at church or if I invite a male friend round for a meal. It irritates me that the underlying assumption is that I am not a complete person without a man, especially as there is no scriptural basis for that.

Amy (28) similarly commented:

Regardless of my desire to be married or not, everyone assumes I both want (yes) and need (I'm not sure) to be married, and that they personally are going to find my husband for me. I also get really peeved when people with whom I don't have an overly close relationship ask, 'So, have you met anyone yet?' and assume they deserve to be told.

Other women felt the pressure towards marriage was implicit rather than explicit:

People in my church don't think there's anything wrong with being single, but I'm sure they'd all love me to turn up with a boyfriend.
Joy, 21

Frances (25) felt that mixed messages were given out about singleness:

I have been taught that singleness is a gift, yet I feel that you are slightly pitied because of it.

Isolation felt in the company of Christian couples or families

Linked to their belief that their singleness was perceived as inferior to marriage was a sense of loneliness and isolation in the presence of couples and nuclear families. Sally (24) wrote about single women's experience of 'feeling like a gooseberry around Christian couples'. As women get older, this isolation may become more acute. Sandra (50) remembered being 'excluded from my peer group as they were all married and socialized together.' Moira (57) commented:

Growing older, with no obvious gifts or skills to offer, and being a relative stranger to some churches, I have experienced the sensation of being 'invisible'. People pass by you in church on their way to speak to their friends, and look through you. When you muster your courage and venture forth to speak to people, they look over your shoulder as you speak, seeking out some person apparently known to them and feigning interest in meeting you, they escape at their earliest opportunity. As a single, middle-aged woman in the evangelical church I have felt marginalized in this way, in more than one church. People seem to have their backs to the door and operate as a social club to themselves.

Lack of ministry opportunities within the church

I don't know where I fit in. I am not seen as someone with very much to offer.

Jennifer, 45

Several women who experienced a lack of encouragement in using their spiritual gifts felt this was connected to dilemmas about how much of a role women are biblically allowed to take on. Tessa (26) had been in environments where women's leadership, preaching, worship leading, prayer-group leading were experienced as dilemmas, as was the issue of whether women should cover their heads when praying and prophesying. Grace (23) wrote:

I have been in church environments, especially in leading holidays and retreats, where I've felt my leadership has been compromised because I'm a girl. The men have generally been unaware of stepping into my realm of authority. This has hindered me being able to develop leadership skills.

Jean (53), who is separated, said: 'Even when married I was never taken seriously in an attempt to dedicate my life to spiritual matters and respond to the call of service to the poor.'

Both Eve (26) and Beth (23) felt that single women were given fewer opportunities in ministry than single men or married couples. Eve added that those with less assertive personalities or those married to spouses who do not attend church are also less likely to receive encouragement. Some older women felt their age was a disadvantage: Georgina (39) was told by a male curate that when she reached the age of forty she would be too old to help with the evangelistic services held for people exploring Christianity for the first time!

Church's unhelpful attitude to dating

Some women thought that the church's emphasis on marriage led to a situation where churches were seen as arenas for husband-hunting. Kitty (21) complained:

> *The negative side of having informal social activities is that church itself becomes a vehicle for flirtation and courtship, and the urgency that many young Christians feel about finding a partner creates a huge distraction from a focused worshipful atmosphere.*

Cressida (27) felt that Christians could be unrealistic in their views about finding a partner. 'Women are starved in waiting for exactly the right person', she wrote, and noted that one church she knew was known popularly by an acronym indicating that it was the place to go to find a partner. Sue (41) likewise felt that churches sometimes hindered the development of relationships:

> *Church is so marriage-orientated and into relationships being handled seriously and responsibly that many churches actually impede relationships happening because people know that the minute they glance at a member of the opposite sex, people will be mentally marrying them off. A more relaxed attitude to dating would take the pressure off people and let relationships happen more naturally.*

Several women commented on disliking being romantically pursued by single Christian men. According to Grace (23):

I have experienced men treating me as of value only as prospective wife, rather than loving me as a sister with absolute purity, and when that happens it absolutely makes my blood boil.

Personal desire for marriage/children

A few women attributed negative experiences in the church to their own desire to marry. Two young women commented:

Sometimes it feels like everyone else is in a great relationship and you're not.

Emily, 20

I find sometimes [singleness] can be viewed as negative by myself as I, and most other Christians I know, put a great deal of pressure on marriage and finding another Christian to spend the rest of your life with.

Miranda, 20

Joy (21), whose church contains many women with babies, admitted that emotionally 'I find the lack of a baby on my knee during the service a lot harder than the lack of a husband by my side!'

Lack of discussion/acknowledgement of issues related to singleness

Tamsin (28) commented:

There is a lack of discussion in relation to singleness and marriage and considering the positives and negatives of both states. If marriage is not considered it can become the ideal. The church needs to be real; people need to be more accountable in who they are in their marriages. Then we could all work together, rather than see things from our own viewpoint.

Christine (54), who is divorced, said:

The church I attend is really a family-orientated church. It simply does not know how to respond. It is my perception that the church does not acknowledge that life in the real world is not how they portray it to be, i.e. full of happy families.

Suzanne (28) feels that the church needs to become more comfortable with discussing 'all sorts of issues related to intimate needs'.

Church teaching about singleness and women's roles

The question 'what teaching (if any) have the churches you've been involved in given on singleness or women's roles?' revealed that four out of ten women had never heard a sermon in church on singleness. A further four out of ten had heard very little preaching on singleness. In total, eight out of ten had received very little or no church teaching on singleness. The remainder had received a limited amount. Only two women in the whole sample had either had regular or frequent teaching on singleness within a whole-church context. Teaching was sometimes conducted in smaller groups: two in ten women said their church had given small-group teaching or a seminar on singleness. These groups tended to be University Christian Unions, youth groups, seminars, or women's days. A few mentioned that seminars on singleness were available at national Christian conferences. A third of the total sample had never been given teaching on singleness in any Christian context.

A third of the women commented on the content of any teaching they had heard. Nine women said that the message given out about singleness had been positive: they were encouraged to view singleness as a gift equal in value to marriage with which one could serve God.

My church generally has one sermon a year on singleness. It views both singleness and marriage positively, I think, and tries to encourage both, recognizing that most of us would like to be married. It has also focused on 'right relationships' in a broader context, and relationships between men and women, which I think has been very helpful and healthy, recognizing that the 'pressure' put on Christian relationships is immense, and I think is partly responsible for the angst that many single people feel when they want to start going out with someone.

Harriet, 30

The basic message was that it was not a 'lesser' state, that everyone should be concentrating on serving God, and that single people should not be constantly 'waiting' for marriage, but that everyone needs to relinquish it to God, and give up the idea of one day being married, regardless of whether it was to be their calling or not. The speaker cited the example of Paul, and how single people are often in a position to serve God more easily/comprehensively than married people who are struggling with the demands and priorities of spouse and family, and that God often has a very specific purpose for single people. However, he was careful not to belittle the fact that God does intend us to marry and reproduce and how from the beginning of creation he saw that it was not good for Adam to be alone, and created Eve to be his companion.

Cheryl, 24

None said that singleness was actively promoted, or was regarded as in any way superior to marriage. Susan (44) felt that her church had neglected the biblical view of singleness being a gift, saying, 'In the 23 years I've been in the church it's never been promoted as a gift, like in the Bible.' Three women had heard issues specifically relating to single women addressed. Where female, rather than male, speakers had given teaching on singleness issues, the women tended to find their teaching much more helpful.

The best thing I went to on singleness was at a college houseparty (all-women's college), with a female speaker. I believe that the spirituality of women is often different to that of men and it is a shame that there is not much of an outlet for it to be developed.

Bethan, 24

Where women made specific comments on the content of single-ness teaching, more had mixed or negative than had positive reactions. A number commented that any teaching on singleness was given as a short 'add-on' or 'flipside' to a sermon on marriage.

> *Singleness is sometimes tagged onto the end of a marriage sermon, giving the example of Paul. That's about it.*
>
> Emily, 20

> *We had a series on Song of Songs, which covered the subjects of marriage and sex, but without much reference to singleness (except in the form: 'If you're not married, this is how it will be when you are ...').*
>
> Annabel, 28

A couple resented the fact that the preacher had been a married man who could not understand single people's perspectives and thus presented singleness simply as a period of waiting to be married. Suzanne (28) described the teaching she had received as 'One hopeless meeting on singleness (led by a vicar in his forties who'd been married since he was 22!) in which singleness was portrayed as a period of marriage preparation.' Jennifer (45) spoke about her recent experience at a large annual Christian conference:

> *I was extremely hurt when attending the only lecture on singleness ... that it was led by a married man who very much assumed that his audience would marry. If you choose to marry only a Christian, then women have a very slight chance of marrying.*

Two women said they would not welcome whole-church teaching on singleness. Hilary (55) felt that 'in a small church it would be very embarrassing to put the focus on certain single people' and suggested single people could attend seminars at conferences or read books on singleness if they wanted to. Two people said that singleness issues were only spoken about to young people, and then in the context of sexuality. Rachel (25) described her reactions to two different church incidents concerning singleness:

> *There was one sermon given at my church on relationships. As part of it, the speaker invited two single people – one man and one woman – to talk for five minutes each on singleness. 'My goodness,' I thought, 'here's a turn up for the books!' but I thought too soon. Both of them basically talked about dating and how to do it! I was livid and outraged! Oooo, it made me cross! However, on another occasion, at the same church, a guy was preaching about something and in the middle of his sermon he asked the marrieds not to pressure the singles about marriage and relationships, particularly when they're going out. I was so thrilled I wanted to stand up and applaud!*

Women's roles were also rarely preached about, although the issue was addressed marginally more frequently than was singleness. Half of the women had received no teaching about women's roles in a whole-church context and two in ten had received very little. In total, seven out of ten of the women who answered the question had received very little or no teaching about women's roles in a whole-church context. A further two in ten said they had been given a small amount of teaching, and less than one in ten had received regular or frequent teaching. Two in ten said teaching on women's issues and roles was available through women's groups or Bible studies. A few had attended national Christian conferences at which the issue had been addressed.

A third of the women talked about the content of the teaching on women's roles. The main theme addressed was related to what women could or could not do within the church. Three women said that they had been taught that men and women could have equal access to all roles within the church.

> *Within the network my church is a part of, there have been many papers and talks about the role of women and encouraging women*

*in leadership. How much churches practise this within the network
varies. Within my church, there are a lot of very strong leading
women, which is positive.*

Tamsin, 28

Three others said they had been taught that women could not
teach the Bible to men or be in authority. Two noted that this
view had been given out subtly, rather than in formal teaching.

*My past churches have taught subliminally, I guess, that women
were to be silent, not have authority. Most telling stuff came out in
annual general meetings … alas, not teaching but diatribe.*

Alex, 27

*I have rarely heard explicit teaching from the pulpit on women's
roles in my current church, but it's there, in a more insidious way. At
festivals/Bible weeks etc., I've heard plenty, mainly based on
extremely poor, lazy theology, and fundamentally misogynistic pre-
suppositions.*

Alice, 29

The next most frequent topic was the role of women in marriage
and women were taught that they should submit to their husbands. Helen (44) summarized the teaching she has received as:
'Women are on earth to support their husbands!'

*Where there has been teaching on women's roles, it's mostly been on
married women's roles and with the underlying understanding that
the man is the head of the household … which doesn't really apply to
single women.*

Sue, 41

Tessa (26) had been taught that women should cover their heads
while praying or giving prophecies. Maggie (30) remembered
hearing a 'very sensitive talk by our pastor' on Mothering
Sunday that took into account the fact that some women do not
have children. Angela (39) explained that she had experienced a

'shift in emphasis' regarding women's roles in the churches she had been involved in:

> *I have in the past been involved in churches which taught very strongly that the man was the head of the household, woman's role was in the home bringing up children, and which refused to let women teach or have any role of authority over men. Having moved churches since then, it is hard to say whether the shift in emphasis has been due to church differences or a general shift in attitudes over time.*

> *The church I am in now has had a number of Ladies' Days, giving teaching on how God uses us as women. This has not been restrictive in any way. It has covered such things as prayer and intercession, prophecy, action (work into the community). It has also had pointers on supporting the men in their work, although I feel we have come a long way from the old house-angel role. The main emphasis has been on getting to know God ourselves and hearing and moving into what he has for us as women.*

Pastoral support for single women

Half of the women were positive about the amount of support available:

> *Absolutely. Pastoral support is available through groups, friends, formal channels through church, regardless of marital status.*
>
> Suzanne, 28

Frances (25) agreed: 'I feel absolutely supported if I need it.' Lisa (31) had received good pastoral support but commented, 'I think the best pastoral support comes through excellent two-way friendship.' Moira (57) felt that in small churches, pastoral support was much easier to access. Paula's (28) church has a 'mentoring system':

You could choose to be partnered with an older woman who is single. There is plenty of pastoral support that is available to all. There is also an annual women's weekend away, which is excellent, and this year was completely done 'in-house' with home-grown speakers etc.

Harriet (30) also has a mentor:

There are counselling networks. I also have a mentor (actually a married woman, but one who understands my career and ambition dilemmas!)

'Our church is strong on small groups and one-to-one discipleship/accountability, which works just as well for single people as it does for marrieds,' said Martha (25). Some women did not think that single women had any specific pastoral needs. 'Pastoral support is available for those who need it, and there seems no reason why single women should need anything special,' said Mary (45). 'Surely we should all be looking out for each other anyway, and there is no need for specific, organized support for single women,' argued Phoebe (25).

One in ten women was unsure or unable to decide whether there was sufficient support. 'You have to fight for it,' remarked Amy (28). 'It varies from church to church,' said Alison (20). 'However, it is definitely something which you have to seek yourself.' 'Depends on the definition of "pastoral support",' said Helen (44). 'My support comes from my friends rather than from a "pastor" '.

Four in ten women were negative about the amount of pastoral support available for single women. Susan (44) said the amount of pastoral support in her church had reduced:

I don't know who the pastors are now ... It depends what sort of problem you've got. The house group I'm in are very much married people with children. There is one other single lady. If I had a problem I might feel I could go to somebody in the group but in the past there've been times when I've worried about things and thought, 'There's just nobody I could go to.' Nowadays, they do offer prayer after each service, which is good, but I'm not the sort of person who would dare go up ,as I'm quite shy.

Valerie (61) felt pastoral needs of single women were varied: 'Widows need particular pastoral care, I feel, and so do one-parent mothers.' Briony (23) wanted more support to be available for single women who struggle with being single: 'It's almost as if people believe you are being very petty if you complain about being single.' Melanie (26) agreed:

> *There also needs to be a proper understanding of the issues involved so that the hurt felt by many women can be properly expressed and dealt with, instead of swept under the carpet.*

Beth (23) said she would appreciate more support on personal issues, for example 'remaining unmarried, coping with illness (mental or physical, e.g. depression to anorexia), relating to men and male authority, ambitions.'

Jude (22) had looked for pastoral support but had not found it:

> *I would really value someone taking the initiative to pastor/disciple me, but it isn't forthcoming. I have taken the initiative a couple of times, but haven't really been followed up by the person.*

In Bethan's (24) experience, women with young children 'have a very strong supportive network, as do the students, but singles who are working would have to make a special appointment with the rector.' Grace (23), who works with female Christian students, felt strongly about the lack of pastoral support for single women:

> *This is one of my main problems. Now I do have pastoral support, but only after looking around and praying for an older woman to meet with for about four years. I have felt a MASSIVE lack of role models in my life, and working with female students all over the UK*

*I see the same thing again and again. I pray that mine will be the last
generation to see such a lack of female role modelling, but it will
mean hard work for those female pastors around.*

A number of women felt there was a need for 'more women's
workers in churches' (Anna, 26), as 'it is not right to always
assume that a vicar's wife will take on an unpaid role of female
pastoral support'. Women who pastor women are often leaders'
wives. Support for women 'could be difficult in churches where
all the leaders are men,' commented Sarah (25), 'but I think
there are usually enough women around who can pastor
women'. She added, however, that 'most of them are married'.
Andrea (28) said, likewise: 'Many in pastoral positions are
married or male and don't fully understand a single woman's
situation.' The church that Mandy (34) belongs to had
considered forming 'ministries to support single women',
although nothing had materialized. Penny (61) saw a need
for 'self-help groups or lunch groups' to be formed. Maggie (30)
was concerned that new people coming into the church
would be put off by the fact that there were no single women
pastors:

*There are positive role models and I get support from my friends
PLUS I do not have a problem approaching my pastor, either for
help or to be referred on. However, I am concerned about the picture
we give to outsiders, because on the service sheets the names are
either male or couples and there are no single female names on the
pastoral team.*

The all-male nature of some church leadership teams posed
problems for Georgina (39):

*The Bishop of [...] wrote to all the clergy in the area suggesting that
they do not meet with single women on their own ... thank you,
Bishop ... I could now feel awkward about discussing matters with
my own vicar, but thankfully he's happy to see me in his office on a
Saturday morning. However, I feel somehow unclean, a woman*

whose moral standards can't be trusted, a bit of a tart ... further separation from the church.

Yet other women would rather not meet with male church leaders on their own and would prefer women pastoral workers.

3

Husband-hunting?

Men, sex and dating

In response to the question: 'What are the main issues facing single Christian women?' issues related to men, sex and dating came second, listed almost as frequently as issues to do with the church's attitude towards them. A quarter of women cited the lack of Christian men as one of the major issues facing single Christian women. There are 'not enough single Christian men to go round!' complained Andrea (28). The Christian men who are still single were described by the women as not 'suitable' (Hilary, 55), 'fanciable' (Miranda, 20), 'decent' (Amanda, 29) or 'godly' (Tanya, 25). 'There seems to be a lack of really nice single Christian men!' said Esther (24). 'Where are all the non-wimp Christian men?' asked Moira (57). Harriet (30) thought that many Christian men were unsuitable because 'they aren't on the same wavelength as Christian women in terms of the way they view the role of women in modern society, let alone the church'. Hilary (55), who is widowed, spoke of 'feeling vulnerable to predatory single Christian men.' Rhiannon (20) agreed that there is a 'danger of men preying on you (!) because they often think you need a man'. Annette (31) had observed 'an increasing reticence on behalf of males in the church to approach [women] to initiate a relationship'. She attributed this to their 'loss of self-esteem while faced with a much more confident and capable generation of women.' The 'possibility that they might never find a partner because there are many more Christian women than men

and it is seen as something bad to marry a non-Christian'
worried Bethan (24).

Whether to date or marry a 'non-Christian' was a dilemma for
a number of women. 'Knowing it is not right to go out with non-
Christians' presents a problem 'for those who do not wish to
spend their life alone', said Briony (23). Annabel (28) spoke
about the difficulty of 'resisting the attraction of non-Christian
men':

*In my experience (though I think it's fairly widespread) it seems that
non-Christian men find something particularly attractive about
Christian women. Not sure why. Even though I am totally per-
suaded that a romantic relationship with a non-Christian isn't an
option, it can still be a huge temptation to give in and enjoy the attention when the opportunity arises.*

Georgina (39) questioned the evangelical belief that it is bad to
marry someone who does not share the same faith:

*What is all this about not settling down with someone who doesn't
share your faith? Catholic women marry non-Christian men and still
get along to Mass and even persuade their unbelieving partner to
send their children to Catholic schools and attend church, so what's
all this taboo in the evangelical church? Why don't we have the same
confidence as our Catholic sisters? Practically, there are more Christian women than men ... what are they supposed to do ...?*

For Frances (25), the attention of non-Christian men in social
and work situations is not always 'respectful'. It results in
women facing the temptation to 'not socialize in a Christian
fashion'. Giving in to such attention may have other negative
consequences. Angela (39) explained:

*For myself, a big issue has been the barrier against looking outside
the church for a partner. Friends who have done this have been
required to leave the church as a result. Some in other churches have
had to battle to be able to take communion.*

Much greater than the dilemma over whether to take an unbelieving partner was the issue of coping with sexual desire. As
Annette and Tamsin explained:

> *I think we underestimate the number of women in the church who
> have been converted as more mature individuals and who have just
> as many struggles with desire for sex and intimacy as their male
> counterparts ... and find that they are a little on the outside, with no
> one to help address these issues.*
>
> Annette, 31

> *Sexual frustrations – sex is not mentioned in church much and so the
> desires of women, especially those who have been in previous rela-
> tionships, is not acknowledged.*
>
> Tamsin, 28

Sexual temptation presents itself, according to Cressida (27), 'via
the media/peers/clothing/socially accepted behaviour ... oh, just
about everything'. Mandy (34) felt that two major issues were:

> *Being excluded from the widespread culture of talking about and
> having sex and being thought strange because of this! How to
> express or enjoy sexuality without being part of the world's view of
> sex.*

A couple of women wondered how to understand Paul's teaching
about marrying if one is 'burning with passion'. Alex (27),
answering the question: 'What are the main issues facing single
Christian women?', replied:

> *For me, probably not having sex! Is that really un-Christian of me to
> admit it? But I've kinda reckoned that the only biblical reason for
> marriage is sex – you know, that 'lest you burn with passion' bit. And
> I am, well, sometimes, burning!*

For Molly (26), sexual frustration can 'possibly lead to guilt,
depression, feeling a failure'. Women who had been married or

had been involved in other sexual relationships missed the sexual and physical intimacy. Hilary (55) felt 'lonely in bed' and noted her 'lack of cuddles'.

Several younger women who are in dating relationships with men were concerned with 'how far is it OK to go' sexually or emotionally outside marriage. They also wondered 'how far "dating" is appropriate' (Kitty, 21). Imogen (23) noted that the line between dating and friendship could be blurred, resulting in 'ambiguous friendships'. Coping with the 'unfulfilled desire to be married' (Tanya, 25) was problematic. Hannah (28) described it as a 'longing' for marriage and a family. Clare (29), who is in full-time Christian work, noted that 'single Christian women in ministry can sometimes feel as if they have shot themselves in the foot for marriage, as they can be seen as a threat to men'. Self-image is an issue for single Christian women, who can wonder, like Rachel (25), 'Does the fact I'm single mean I'm unattractive?' Hannah (28) spoke of 'feeling like I should look like Ally McBeal'. Bethan (24) recognized that being single does not mean a woman is unattractive. To have a 'negative self-image' is 'ridiculous, as the older single women at my church are some of the most attractive'. Tessa (26) was concerned about how Christian women should dress, Bethan (24) with how to cope with 'broken hearts'.

Desire for marriage

The vast majority of the women in the sample (eight out of ten) want to marry. Of 76 women who answered the question: 'Would you like to get married?' 60 said they would, 10 said they were undecided and 6 said they would not. Younger women tended to be more certain of a desire to marry than older women, some of whom had experienced divorce or widowhood, or, if they had never married, had observed other people's marriages over the years and were put off. Younger women also had more idealistic expectations of marriage. Of those who answered yes, a quarter added provisos such as, 'in the future', 'if I met the right person' or, 'if God wants me to'. Tina (35), who is divorced, added, 'I think my daughter would like me to get married again!' Bethan (24), who has a divorced friend, said she was a little wary because 'it would be worse to marry someone who left you'. Emily (20) said she would 'like to feel "sorted" first, or on the road to becoming so. Which is probably tied up with not wanting to be like my mother'. Amy (28) pointed out that although she wants to marry, 'I don't want to get married at all costs – as someone else said, "I'd rather be single and wish I were married than married and wish I were single".'

Three-quarters of women added reasons as to why they wanted to marry. The most commonly cited reason was the desire for 'companionship', 'sharing', 'intimacy' and protection from loneliness. Some described the marriage partnership in terms of 'enjoyment', 'fun', 'romance' and 'celebration'. 'All gifts from God to be enjoyed', summarized Frances (25). The second most common reason was desire for children. After this came reasons to do with serving God and growing as a Christian. Fourth came desire for sexual activity. Other less popular reasons included laziness, desire for security and the positive example of parents' marriages. 'I want somebody else to tell me what to do!' said Carolyn (23); 'so that my husband can earn lots of money and I don't have to go to work any more!' joked Melanie (26); 'I've seen the way my parents have partnered together as a real team serving God, and I really want to be part of something like that,' said Amy (28).

Sophie and Hazel want to marry because of a desire for companionship:

Interesting question, ask myself every day! Spiritual answer: Desire of my heart. Emotional answer: Want to share my life with my 'soul mate'. Worldly answer: Tired of being on my own.

Sophie, 31

I want to share myself completely with my potential husband (the true meaning of sacrificial love) – mentally, physically and spiritually and although I don't think it right or fair that he be seen as someone

who can fulfil all my desires, it goes that one step deeper into sharing
the intimacies and mysteries of what I believe God intends.

Hazel, 32

Marriage was strongly linked to fulfilment (emotional, physical and spiritual) in quite a few of the women's responses. Although some noted, like Hazel (above), that a husband could not 'fulfil all my desires', women had high expectations of the fulfilment to be gained from marrying.

I want to get married because I desperately want to share my life
with the 'right man'. It sounds so naff, and I know a lot of women
who feel the same, but I have such an enormous capacity to love and
be loved! So do we all, I suppose. I love the balance that you some-
times see in couples; men who understand their identity in Christ and
are therefore free to be 'real' men (not in some trite, macho way),
amazingly complemented by a strong and feminine woman! (Of
course, according to people's own colourful personalities; I really
don't mean in a superficial way). I would love to be in a partnership
like that. And I would love to have a family one day. I think that
however fulfilled I might be in my career, and even, ideally, in my
relationship with God and friends and family, I don't think I would
feel completely fulfilled if I never got to be a wife and mother.
(Dodgy?!) I must say, though, if I do not meet someone who I know
is right for me, then I will not compromise.

Cheryl, 24

Sue (41) saw marriage as the solution to the strains of our 'mobile society':

Sooner or later, friends and friendships move on because we live in a
mobile society. The friendships don't disappear but the immediacy
and day-to-day relevance of them does when someone moves away.
I'd really like to have a permanent relationship that won't disappear
when someone moves away to a new job or something. Someone to
share the day-to-day things with, share my future and my plans with,
someone who's rooting for me on a day-to-day basis and who I can
root for.

Jean (53) was the only person who envisaged an alternative form of partnership to heterosexual marriage:

> *It would be good to share one's life with someone like-minded. However, it does not need to be a man and I suppose one does not need to marry.*

Desire for children was strong for many of the women who wanted to marry:

> *Marriage brings the possibility of children – big factor in its favour! Having an opportunity to be a mother is very important to me.*
>
> Beth, 23

> *I would also like to have a family at some point, and, as a Christian, the marriage thing has to come first!*
>
> Esther, 24

> *On a practical level, I would also like to have a family and believe that children need the support and love of two parents, not one. Artificial insemination is not an option for me, as I do not believe it to be the best, either for myself or my potential children.*
>
> Hazel, 32

> *I would like to get married and have kids, and because of my age, time is running out, so it's not quite a desperation but it feels like it's got to happen soon or it's not going to happen.*
>
> Anita, 36

Some felt being married would enable them to serve God better than they could as singles:

> *Having someone always there for encouragement, especially to spur me on in godliness and Christian living, and to be able to spur him on, too. Being able to support someone else's ministry, in the hope that two of us working together might be more effective than individually.*
>
> Annabel, 28

I reckon you can hit people with the gospel better working as a team.
Rhiannon, 20

Two women believed that it was God's plan for them. Amanda (29) said:

> To fulfil God's plan for my life (assuming it is) – because I believe that God has someone special for me who shares my passions and dreams and with whom I will be able to operate more fully to serve him in every way.

Two thought working at marriage would help them 'grow in godliness'. As is evident in Cheryl's response (above), a number of women wanted the experience of complementarity they saw as most evident in Christian marriage. Tessa (26), who has a boyfriend, expressed this in two of her reasons:

> e) Because I can see, in the relationship I am in now, and in examples of Christian marriage around me, how good and how fun it is for two people of the opposite sex to be in such a close and constant relationship, in a way that is different from two Christian friends of the same sex.

> f) Because I think this is essentially how God has made us to be – to leave our parents and to be joined to another person of the opposite sex, and to live life with each other, complementing each other's differences.

Paula (28) said she wanted to 'explore my femininity in relationship to a man' and that marriage was the most obvious place to do this. A few other women alluded to the book of Genesis:

> I think that most people feel an internal urge to pair off with someone and most women feel the urge to have children at some stage. I realize this is a generalization, but I think it is true. I would like to have children and the security of marriage. I also feel a need to support someone, which I think could be inbuilt by God. After all, in

Genesis the woman was created to be a helper for the man. I think (and this is just a personal theory) that women are created with a desire and ability to serve and help others, particularly marriage partners.

Anna, 26

Several mentioned a desire to model Christ's relationship with the church. Kitty (21) commented that marriage

is a (very human) model of his own yearning for relationship, and of the mutual self-sacrifice and joyful union of Christ and his church. Too many people see that union in abstract terms, but when it is crystallized by a comparison with the marriage covenant it takes on far deeper, authentic meanings.

Marital sex was another factor in favour of marriage:

Sex, quite simply – it's a physical instinct to want to make love, and I don't really want to have to suppress it for the rest of my life.

Carolyn, 23

Christine (54), who is divorced, said she misses having sex. Sue (41) would like 'a sexual relationship and someone to be able to touch in a meaningful way.'

Cressida (27), after listing the reasons why she wanted to marry, mused that desire for marriage was an 'attempt at reaching heaven on earth':

We talk about being the bride of Christ ... being accepted for who we are, being loved in a way no human can offer ... and that is the ultimate commitment leading us to heaven. I guess marriage is our small attempt at reaching heaven on earth.

Those who were undecided as to whether they wanted to marry tended to be older. Valerie (61) commented:

I wouldn't be too easy to live with! On the other hand, if the Lord very definitely showed me this was for me, then I would go with it

200 per cent. But there would have to be a lot of chemistry flowing around!

Maggie (30) has become used to being single: 'I have been single for so long and have regarded marriage as something which may happen, but if it doesn't then God will take care of me in that regard. Not being married is not something that worries me.' Penny (61), who is a widow, would only remarry 'if I was very sure that I could make the readjustments that would be necessary'.

All the women who said they did not want to marry were aged over thirty. There are a number of possible reasons for this. Perhaps social pressure to desire marriage is stronger for younger women; perhaps singleness becomes easier and more enjoyable as women get used to living a single adult life; perhaps, as they age, women become more realistic about their diminished opportunities for marriage; or perhaps they witness sufficient unhappy marriages (either their own or others') to understand that marriage does not fulfil in the way they once imagined.

I can't imagine meeting a guy that I would be happy to give up my single life for!

Fiona, 32

I don't want to get married at all now. I think there are so many problems in so many marriages that it's very hard to find a very happy marriage ... It's a fight between the temperaments and when you're not feeling well and you've got work to do I just think [being single] is so much easier. I don't have shirts to iron and if I don't feel like doing anything I can just have a quick sandwich and I don't have to prepare a meal and bother about other people's wants and wishes ... It's a bit selfish, isn't it!

Barbara, 65

I've had a go, enjoyed some of the fruits, been shaped to a degree by the consequences of it. Although I enjoy the company of men, I have no desire for the intimacy of marriage; this may be because I feel too old for it.

                                                                    Moira, 57

Although Ivy (78) never made an active choice not to marry, looking back on her life she is glad she did not marry. Being single allowed her to dedicate herself to looking after abandoned children:

> *I remember thinking once ... I was no longer young and I was messing about with my waifs and strays, and there was a little possibility of a husband coming along. I always remember thinking, 'Do you know, I wouldn't be able to do this if I had a husband.'*

Fiona (32) related an encounter with a married man who questioned her singleness:

> *I met a bloke once (he was about sixty and typical of a lot of people of his generation!) who couldn't understand 'why a lovely young thing like you isn't married' ... we chatted about the fact that I was happy as I was and he gave me a really hard time about it. Then I asked him if he was happy in his marriage. 'Hell, no, it's awful,' he said. He really couldn't see that he was encouraging me to do something that was making him completely miserable! There are so many miserable married people out there, but most of them think we should be married too! Can't understand why! Maybe they want us to join the suffering, too! Or maybe they just want us to fulfil what they see as normal!*

Asked if they were actively trying to find a partner, one in ten said yes, two in ten said they were sometimes, or were 'on the lookout', and six in ten said they were not. The remaining one in ten had boyfriends. Methods of trying to find a partner included involvement with different Christian organizations and church groups, going to Christian balls and dance classes, socializing with other Christians, praying, and using a Christian dating service.

I used to have a 'criteria list'... Every time I met someone new, I'd try to match them up against my criteria, to find out if they could be 'the one'... My whole purpose in life almost became trying to find Mr Criteria. I wouldn't say I'm actively trying to find a partner at the moment, because I know that when I start to do this, my focus goes away from God. I trust him that if someone comes along who would make me a good husband, it will be clear to me without me having to go and put lots of effort into analysing every man I ever come across.

Joy, 21

A friend of mine has recently got engaged ... As far as I was concerned, he went about the whole thing in completely the wrong way ... So when the news of their engagement came through, I was seriously concerned. However, the more I've thought and prayed about it, the more sobering home truths I've learned about myself. I realized that I thought that one had to reach some kind of perfect understanding of relationships and state of total contentment with one's singleness, that you had to have said to the Lord, 'OK, I am now perfectly happy to spend the rest of my days as a single person' and really mean it and then AND ONLY THEN the Lord would say, 'Congratulations! You've made it, you're now ready for marriage, here have a spouse ...' To my horror, I have realized that I have wasted a ridiculously large amount of time looking for the marriage formula, trying to be, say and do the right things with God so that he'd deem me ready for my husband. When have I EVER done ANYTHING that deserved ANY of the blessings that God has bestowed upon me throughout my life? And what am I trying to say? That married people are perfect and have made it and single people aren't and haven't? And in my attempts to secure a future husband, am I thinking that marriage is the ultimate, perfect, happy state?...The grass is only green when you water it. For a start, I cannot manipulate God. He is very secure and besides, my entire thinking displays a complete lack of understanding of the nature of God. I need to give up, stop looking for formulas and trust him that what he's given me right now is all I need and that he 'has plans to prosper and not to harm me, plans to give me hope and a future', whatever that holds in store. Above all, I need to relax and simply be myself. Since this revelation, life has become much easier and far more enjoyable!

Rachel, 25

Dating agencies

Dating agencies are becoming a more accepted way of finding a partner, both in contemporary society and in Christian circles. The question: 'What do you think about Christian dating agencies?' sought to discover how widespread is the approval of dating agencies. Three out of ten women said they were positively disposed towards them, or would consider using them. The women whose views were most positive tended to be older. Six women from the sample said they had used one in the past, although most were negative about the experience. Three out of ten said they were ambivalent or unsure. Four out of ten expressed a negative attitude or would not consider using one.

Fiona (32) joined an agency when she was twenty-seven:

I was really happy being single, but thought that I might not always be and ought to at least have a bit of a look. It was very enlightening and I went out with some great blokes. In the end, it only served to confirm my suspicions that I really was very happy being single and that I should stay that way.

Sue (41) was positive about the existence of dating agencies, but had a few reservations:

I have tried one. I think it's a good idea in principle but I think there are probably better, more natural ways to facilitate relationships happening. I'd far rather get to know someone as a friend in a social situation, but the minute you join an agency, you are already setting your stall out and I think it does force you into making some instant first judgements. On the other hand, we are a minority group and probably need systems to facilitate meeting potential partners.

Christine (54) was considering joining one but 'I ... dread the sort of Christian men I might find.' Angela (39) has tried a couple but found 'they seem to attract geeks'. Jennifer (45) approached several agencies but discovered 'they are extremely top heavy for women and the age groups are generally not encouraging'. Paula (28) had attended a large Christian singles ball:

> *Naff is my first reaction to going to a [...] ball which had poor ambiance and put on slow dances at 10.30 pm. I'm sure there is potential in them, but you'd have to be pretty thick-skinned to the cheesiness of it all.*

Quite a few supported the idea of dating agencies in principle but felt it 'wasn't for them'. Jude (22) said using an agency would 'make me feel like a freak', continuing:

> *I think that blokes going through dating agencies are probably a bit weird (even though that sounds a bit mean!) because all the nice Christian blokes have no trouble finding a partner (especially with there being more Christian men than women).*

'Ghastly,' exclaimed Nancy (45):

> *I would not marry someone just because they were a Christian. They're usually the worst kind of men; they use their Christianity as a way of getting your trust. OR they hide behind it because they are peculiar men (sorry!). With so many spare women in the church, men who need dating agencies cannot be up to much.*

Quite a few women used strong language to express their disapproval, saying, 'Eek!', 'Cheesy', 'Ugh', 'No way!' and 'Run a million miles from them!' 'I would rant and rave at the thought, because Paul says, "If you're single, DON'T LOOK FOR A WIFE"' said Grace (23), then adding, 'But I have heard that God can really use them, and who am I to curse what God chooses to bless?' Harriet (30) had strong feelings against them:

> *UURGHHH!!! I cannot tell you how strongly the concept of the Christian dating agency appals me! I would rather be single than go*

*through such a process to meet someone. It's an unnatural context,
with undue pressure. It also, I think, encourages singles to dwell on
their loneliness and desire to get married rather than be content with
where they're at, trust God, and get on with life in the meantime. I
have friends who have joined [a Christian dating agency] and I am
sure it has made them more unhappy with being single than they
were before!*

Younger women were less positive about dating agencies. Cheryl
(24) saw them as a 'last resort':

*As a means for Christian men and women to meet, I think they are –
in some ways – a good idea, and I think it is naïve to think that you
can lock yourself in an ivory tower and God will still bring your
Prince Charming. For me, at the moment, though, the thought is
anathema! It seems to take so much of the romance out of it to have
to search so frenetically, and I do believe God will be preparing me
for someone specific (and vice versa). I am trusting him for that.
However, if I got to my mid-thirties and was not married and had
found no one, I'm sure I would not turn my nose up at meeting
Christians through dating agencies. However, I would expect –
unfortunately – to meet very few 'normal' people. It would definitely
be a last resort for me.*

A number of women were against dating agencies because they
felt they represented a failure to trust God to find them a partner
if he wants them to have one. 'I don't believe in them at all. God
will provide meetings of people he wants to unite,' replied Briony
(23). 'I think it implies a lack of trust in God's ability to provide
and direct in our lives,' said Melanie (26). Others said they
thought trying to 'force a relationship' was unhelpful and that
friendship was the best way to find a man. Lorna (51) saw them
as a potentially useful way of meeting people but also believed
that 'they can add to the pressure that some single women feel
that they have no real identity or value unless they find a man'.
Denise (23) thought dating agencies could be 'useful if you are
in a situation where you don't meet people naturally', but

cautioned that they 'run the risk of not seeing singleness as the gift it is and subscribing to the modern notion of love'. Sandra (50) commented on their existence in contemporary society as a sign of widespread loneliness:

> *I think they can play a part, but probably because our culture makes us so isolated and busy that we need artificial help, like dating agencies. They can devalue people, and turn relating to brothers and sisters into shopping for the perfect outfit.*

Eve (26) thought that dating agencies could foster an unhealthy preoccupation with finding a partner, adding 'being too desperate can result in an unhappy marriage, which, in my view, is worse than being single.' Maggie (30) knows someone who runs a Christian dating agency and admires its work:

> *I do not have a problem with them if the focus is on God – it worries me if people think a special someone will fill a gap which only God can and it must be appreciated that people in relationships can also get lonely.*

Sex and sexuality

The most common complaint was that Christians do not talk openly about sex and sexuality issues. Any teaching given by church leaders is restricted to the message: 'Don't have sex outside marriage.' While marital sex is celebrated in church environments, sexual desire felt by singles is either ignored or assumed to be bad. Little practical advice is given as to how to view and handle sexual desire, and whether genital expression, such as masturbation, is acceptable for Christians. Widespread Christian myths about women's lack of interest in sex are proved false by the women's responses. A high number of women reported struggling with sexual desire. Some said they wished they could discuss and examine the issue with other single Christian women, perhaps in a women's group.

There was much uncertainty as to what sexuality is: whether 'sexuality' refers simply to the gender of the person one is attracted to, whether it just resides in one's genitals or whether it is integral to the human person. 'Do I have any?' asked Jennifer (45), 'I thought I was invisible.' Denise (23) commented: 'There are times when I think that sexuality is irrelevant for a single person but sometimes I think that sexuality is a much more fundamental part of how we act.' Sylvia (72) saw it in the context of the whole person: 'We're not just sexual organs. We've got minds as well as bodies, and spirits. I wouldn't take sexuality out of the context of a whole life.' Nancy (45) believes 'we are all sexual creatures':

> *One has to indwell one's sexuality. I believe in non-physical intimacy. This may involve being quite flirtatious, etc. Suppressing entirely one's sexuality in the interests of some odd notion of purity is psychologically disastrous. I made that mistake myself for some years, because I had had bad teaching about sex as being wrong in itself. I believe absolutely that sex outside marriage is wrong: very damaging all round.*

Almost all the women agreed that sex was best left for marriage and that they aimed to 'stay pure'. However, this was not always easy.

> *I still (just about) maintain the view that sex is for marriage. However, I find celibacy extremely difficult to stick with. I find it extremely annoying that God has given us a desire for sex, and restricted it to marriage. I can understand why this is so, but it is frustrating when you don't have a marriage partner, and cannot see having one in the near future.*
>
> Molly, 26

> *Dealing with desire can be difficult, obviously to varying degrees, depending on the person and situation. I find that giving it all to God in theory is great, but tough in practice – it's almost a case of casting your burdens at the Lord's feet, and then trying to carry them yourself a short while later.*
>
> Ruth, 23

Tanya (25), likewise, saw singleness as a state in which one could not fully express sexuality: 'God created us, therefore we are sexual beings. We just can't express it fully,' she said.

> It's something that isn't talked about much … I sometimes think people want to think that as a single person (especially a single woman) you are somehow asexual, which is, of course, absolute tosh. Or if they acknowledge it is an issue, they think that it is dealt with by saying 'don't'. However, when you are single, it is something that is there day in, day out, and is a choice day in and day out. It doesn't get any easier with time.
>
> Sue, 41

Some women called for an acknowledgement of their sexuality. 'Single women have sexual feelings!' exclaimed Moira (57), 'even though they rarely talk about it. Knowing how to channel those feelings is an art form. The church needs to address these issues with some urgency.' Angela (39), while believing sex outside marriage is wrong, wanted the church to have greater compassion for people who fail in this area:

> I do think the church needs to tread a very fine path between not encouraging promiscuity and laying really heavy guilt trips on people for every mistake they make, and I feel they still fall strongly on the side of the guilt.

'The church has a lot to work through in relation to sexuality,' thought Sian (41). 'The issues of homosexuality and divorce seem to be the two unforgivable sins!' Kitty (21) wanted Christians to be more realistic about the fact that Christians do have sexual experiences:

> Prayer support and unconditional forgiveness should be offered by friends and churches, as well as practical advice and teaching.

Not all the women struggled with sexual temptation. For Joy (21), who has never had a sexual relationship, temptation to masturbate was there when she was in her teenage years, but she resisted and now finds abstinence easy. Amy (28) had found abstinence fairly easy, which she attributes to never having dated anyone 'and therefore never [having] been in a situation to be tempted to the point of actually having sex.' She still feels she knows 'next to nothing' about sex:

> We hardly ever talked about it in my family ... For most of my life, I haven't bothered to find out more, because I figured that would make it more of an issue and harder to deal with, so I just didn't want to be bothered. Probably some of my sexuality was stifled in its development (or however you want to describe that), and so I've only become more seriously interested, and wanted to have sex at all, in the past few years.

Some women felt that men have greater struggles with sexual desires, but others saw this as a myth. 'I feel it's as much of an issue as for men,' said Tessa (26). 'Women may seek sexual experiences just as much as men, but for other reasons – e.g. to feel loved, for a feeling of intimacy.'

> I have several Christian friends who really struggle with sexual desires (particularly if they have had previous sexual relationships before becoming Christians). It's hard for them because the desire for intimacy is gripping ... but there's no way of satisfying that, other than hooking up with a non-Christian, which many of them give in to. And because sexuality is quite often associated with identity ... these are huge issues that are just swept under the carpet and not dealt with. I guess that they can start to feel a little androgynous. I know that I have felt that in the past. There is little understanding (particularly in our sex-driven culture) that helps single women understand that they are still sexual beings despite the fact that they aren't married or having sex. By not addressing the issue, we let it go underground and women get desperate for an affirmation of their sexuality and then get themselves into all sorts of trouble. The number of women that I know that are/have been sexually active in our congregation is a little scary, even those in leadership. Not

helped either by Christian boyfriends putting pressure on them to
sleep with them.

Annette, 31

Annette was not the only one to mention that numbers of single
Christian women do become involved in sexual relationships.
Women become sexually involved not because they believe it is
right to do so, but because of the inability to overcome temptation in dating relationships. Grace (23), who has herself been in
this situation, said:

> *I know of very few who've managed not to sleep with boyfriends,*
> *but also very few who think that it's OK to. Those who have tend to*
> *be the most adamant that we shouldn't. I think a lot of fault lies with*
> *the nature of 'going out' relationships. As Christians, it seems we*
> *think the bed is the only place to be different, but people get so*
> *intense emotionally ...*

Those who said they had experience of sexual relationships
found abstinence particularly hard. 'The fact that I have developed a taste for the vine's fruits makes it that much harder to
abstain!' commented Cressida (27).

Those who referred to lesbianism said that it was not biblically permissible. Like Anna (26) they believed 'lesbianism is not
an option from the Bible's point of view'. Briony (23) acknowledged that some Christian women struggle with same-sex
attraction:

> *I think a lot of Christian women are tempted to have relationships*
> *with other Christian women simply because there are not enough*
> *men around and women understand other women much better than*
> *men anyway. It's easy to cross the line between very close friendship*
> *and inappropriate actions.*

References to masturbation tended to be veiled. Where it was
mentioned, some said they did not believe it was appropriate
behaviour for Christians:

Women are sexual beings, with a sex drive. I believe it to be inappropriate to manifest this in any physical way (homo- or heterosexual genital activity or masturbation – although the latter is better than driving yourself crazy!) or through fantasy. Seems a bit of a hard line, but I think we need to trust God to know us better than we know ourselves sometimes.

Yvonne, 31

Hilary (55) disagreed:

There is no point feeling guilty if one has erotic dreams, or needs to masturbate, or is stimulated by a romantic film. We must acknowledge that we are human. We should, however, be able to talk about all things with Jesus. Hidden thoughts and fantasies and practices can never be hidden from him and our relationship with Jesus is spoiled if we try to hide anything.

Grace (23) recalled the only time she heard female masturbation addressed from the pulpit, by a young male speaker:

After saying he and his mates are accountable about 'Tommy', he said he wondered what the female euphemism was. The congregation actually gasped. SO ridiculous. I guess one explanation is that while girls go 'yuck' at the thought of boys masturbating, boys tend to get turned on if it's the other way around and girls still go 'yuck'.

Rachel (25) felt that sexual energy could be 'channelled into other things' and recommended dancing as one solution! Nancy (45) and Moira (57) saw their 'channelled' sexual energy as a benefit in the development of their talents and ministry:

Becoming a Christian was the single most important thing that happened in learning to control my sexuality. It was the gateway to a life where I was not at the mercy of my emotions and lusts! I learned to channel my energies purposefully into developing my talents and opportunities, and so sexuality was pivotal to my 'character reconstruction' after my conversion, if you like.

Nancy, 45

My sexuality, offered up, should give power and a special fruitful-
ness to my ministry.

Moira, 57

A few women had had to explain to non-Christian men that
they could not start a relationship with them because of differing
views on sex.

One guy felt that he couldn't go out with me because he knew that I
wouldn't have sex outside of marriage – it was a real struggle, as I
longed to go out with him and it was very tempting, therefore, to give
in, but again God gave me the strength to overcome that.

Clare, 29

Ruth (23) found it 'hard to explain my abstinence, and the
reasons for it, to some non-Christians, as premarital sex is
almost expected in society'. Esther (24) was relieved to be free of
the pressure to become immediately sexually involved with a
boyfriend:

I am so glad to be free of the pressure of non-Christian relationships,
where it is totally the norm to be in bed on the first date. I have a
(male) friend who was saying that every time he meets a girl he
expects to be asked about sex within about two weeks. As a Chris-
tian, he finds this really awkward, and is trying really hard to meet a
'nice Christian girl' who won't behave in such a standard-behaviour
way.

A substantial number of women called for a greater acknowledgement and discussion of sexual issues among Christians.
Ruth (23) concluded:

I think that the problem for single Christian women with regard to
sexuality is primarily that there is no support, help and not much
good Christian literature on the subject. It's not talked about, and
therefore feelings and desires can be seen as wrong. It can all be quite
confusing!

Emotional issues

Emotional issues connected to singleness came third in order of importance for single Christian women. The most significant emotional issue was fear of the future and, in particular, of a future which did not hold marriage. 'Whether God wants them to stay single or get married one day' is, according to Catherine (19), 'a big question many Christian women ask themselves, as God's will for us should be the most important thing in our lives'. Emily (20) wondered, 'Is it God's plan for me to get married? If so, who's the guy?' Fear was an issue almost exclusively for women under thirty. Women feared remaining single, not fulfilling their parents' expectations, loneliness, growing old alone. Frances (25) feared 'being thirty and still being single'. Miranda (20) predicted that fear of remaining single could lead to marrying an unsuitable partner. There is a 'danger of making do with second best because of a fear you'll never meet anyone else', she said. Becky (23) thought that being married was necessary for achieving happiness and questioned 'whether [single women] can trust God with their future, whether he has their happiness in his plans, or should they go and find themselves a partner because they dare not wait'. Although Melanie (26) acknowledged that 'God has a good plan for my life', she realized that 'let's face it, there are more women than men in the church!'

Although some women feared remaining single, some recognized that they needed, as Nikki (20) explained, to keep their desire to marry 'under control so that God, and not a relationship, is still number one'. Rhiannon (20) had noticed a 'temptation to be distracted from God by the "hunt" for a man, even seeing church as a kind of dating agency'. Yvonne (31) felt single women faced the challenge 'not to become selfishly single'. They need to deal with their 'inability to trust God' (Molly, 26). In addition to fearing remaining single, some women feared not having children. Rachel (25) and Carrie (30) pointed out that since women's fertile years are fewer than men's, this increased the urgency of their desire for children.

Several women spoke of the need to remain content in their present situation. Annabel (28) commented:

> *It's easy to feel discontented about being single at the best of times, whether Christian or not. There's a great temptation to imagine that life would be better if I was married, even though I'm sure it's just as hard, only different! This feeling is often reinforced by the attitude of some other Christians (usually male and married!) that the best thing that could happen to a single Christian woman would be to get married!*

Hazel (32) and Cheryl (24) noted the issue of rejection, defined by Cheryl as 'struggling not to come under perceived rejection from God, men, other people'. Two women worried about lacking the 'spiritual covering' of a man. Hilary (55), who is widowed, said:

> *I found being married to a super Christian man gave me spiritual covering, and a stability. I'm praying that my views don't get out of line with the Lord's revealed will.*

Other emotional issues encountered included 'making sure that going to church doesn't become a social activity because you are single and appreciate new friendships' (Paula, 28), 'self-esteem' (Hannah, 28 and Jude, 22), 'psychological health' (Sandra, 50) and gender identity: 'finding a way to be freely feminine and yet independent and strong' (Hannah, 28).

Life in contemporary society

Living in contemporary society was the last most frequently cited issue for single Christian women. The women who noted this as an issue tended to be older, which would indicate that, had the sample for this book been more representative of older women, practical dilemmas of life would have figured more highly. Within this category, the greatest concern was career-related.

In many ways, the issues are the same for all single women in this generation – career management and discrimination, maintaining self-confidence/self-esteem in an age when to be 'worth something' is to have 'achieved' in the eyes of the world, juggling our need for relationships (both romantic, family and others) with the demands of work (long hours, intensity).

Harriet, 30

Annette (31) commented on the danger that if single women's gifts are not recognized or used within church life, this will result in them 'looking for recognition of their gifts/talents in the secular workplace'. Her own early church experience led her to pursue a career because 'I found that in the workplace, I was respected for my gifts, abilities and intelligence ... which sadly I found lacking in the church.' Bridget (43) thinks that 'professional women over thirty' are not recognized or accepted by the church. Yvonne (31) wanted to 'inform the church at large that it is not very good at being in touch with society's relatively positive view of women and their careers'. Georgina (39) painted a picture of the life of such a woman:

Well, of course [women] could stay single for the kingdom and get involved with their evangelical church – after all, they have so much time ... after their demanding job with possibly long hours, after they've gone to the supermarket, cooked tea, put the washing in the machine, done the hoovering, washed up, emptied the bins, decorated the spare bedroom, mowed the lawn, pruned the bushes, chatted to the lady next door, slogged up to [Christian dance classes] in search of a mate, organized a social life nearer to home (no one's going to do it for you), sorted out a friend's crisis, applied for ten jobs because your company is going through a bad patch and there are rumours of redundancies being imminent ... then, yes, you could get involved with activities at your local evangelical church ... I'm usually ready for bed after all that!

Three women were concerned about finances. Beryl (64) complained about pension provision:

A number of years ago, I had a breakdown and was retired on the grounds of ill health. At the time I was working and had been receiving half pay and invalidity benefit. My benefit was stopped before my pension came through. Thus, there was a time when I had no money coming in at all. I did ring the inquiry line and explained the situation and that I lived with my parents, who are both OAPs, to be told that I could not claim anything, as I was unable to work full-time.

Jennifer (45) was worried about a number of financial issues:

Financially, life is very tight, as I live in one of the most expensive places in the country but without the matching salary. I have still not got a mortgage because I cannot work any more hours and am about £50,000 short of buying a one-bedroomed flat. My pension is also a real worry. The social housing policy on single households is appalling, too. I dread my old age as at present I will be financially very poor, be forced to move and will be unable to provide funds for private nursing should the need arise.

Hilary (55) noted that single women face 'having to look after all the DIY jobs oneself', as well as doing car maintenance and worrying about 'personal safety issues of being in the house alone and going out at night'. Both Jennifer (45) and Molly (26) commented on difficulties with holidays:

There's the financial implications of the break and the single supplements which are added, but there is also the mental break of having to take time away from routine when you can be very lonely. Also, on a practical point, you are often seen as the one person in an organization who will work the bank holidays because you haven't got a family. That means that you end up with time off when your friends have gone back to work.

Jennifer, 45

4

Attitudes

The Bible and single women

Since the women had received little Christian teaching on singleness (see Chapter 2), how far had they themselves looked into
biblical teaching on singleness, or biblical examples of single
women? What did they understand to be a biblical view of singleness, and how did this affect their lives as single women? The
answers to the question: 'What would you say is a biblical view
of singleness for women?' were varied. A large number of
women described singleness as a 'gift', 'calling', 'vocation', as
something which is 'positive', 'fine', 'good', 'honourable', 'appropriate', 'fulfilled', 'all right' or 'OK'. Fewer than one in ten
women describing it as a gift expressed an understanding that
singleness was in any sense 'better' than marriage, although they
recognized that singleness could enable women to do more to
serve God.

> *It can be a blessing, as for Paul, to remain pure and holy, to trust God
> with our lives – he is in control.*
>
> Sally, 24

> *A very positive one. Currently I am a eunuch for the kingdom of
> heaven (Jesus), and not being distracted from my pursuit of God by a
> man.*
>
> Sarah, 25

We should use singleness to serve God more fully than perhaps a married-with-kids woman could, and we should use singleness to grow closer to/become more reliant upon God.

Emma, 22

Both singleness and marriage are gifts. Whether our status changes at some point or not, we need to relish the 'gift' we have now, and serve God with everything we are in that.

Amy, 28

I don't see it as different from a view of singleness for men. It is clear that there is a call to singleness for the purposes of ministry – which some feel. My experience is that the majority of single folk do not feel called to that singleness. I would nevertheless see Scripture as presenting every life experience – including finding oneself as single – as something to be taken up in a positive way. I would see a 'biblical view' as encouraging single people to recognize and enjoy the benefits of their singleness, recognize and accept the disadvantages and, within the context they find themselves, to live their lives seeking to serve God in the context of community (i.e. to recognize that singleness does not prevent the interdependence which Christian life affirms).

Lorna, 51

A number thought that singleness was for the minority of people.

It is for the few who are specially selected and it is honourable to be single. But for the most, we were made to have partners.

Cressida, 27

I would say that it is a definite calling for some people, but just because of the way that human nature is, it is clearly not for everyone, or the majority. How are we to 'people the earth'? It is hugely significant that God created Eve for Adam, and that he has created us with this innate need/urge to reproduce.

Cheryl, 24

Several commented that in the Bible, identity does not reside in a person's marital status but in her status as a Christian. For the Christian, her relationship with God is more significant than any other relationship.

I don't think the Bible encourages us to make our singleness (or our marriage) the primary thing that defines us, but we have a tendency to do just that.

Annabel, 28

God created each of us to be in relationships, but no human relationship or marriage will ever be more than the dimmest reflection of the friendship which each one of us can enjoy with God when we accept his forgiveness. That friendship and the forgiveness draw no distinction between single people and attached people. At the same time, the ways in which they manifest themselves in our lives are different between single people and attached/married people, so both singleness and marriage should be treasured as the good gifts that they are.

Carolyn, 23

I see the general message to single women as to all people … Jesus is our Husband, our Lover, and all our needs and desires can be fulfilled in Him. Also, he is in control, and can provide a husband, if he wants to. Also, we are all one in Christ, and we have the same Holy Spirit in us as married women and single/married men, and can therefore have an equal relationship with God and ministry as married women/single or married men.

Tessa, 26

In terms of biblical portrayals of single women, few women gave specific examples. Some remarked that single women were looked down upon in the Old Testament and that women were expected to be married. Some pointed out that the Bible gives considerable attention to widows and urges the church community to care and provide for them. A few noted Jesus' approval of single women and listed examples of single female New Testament characters.

It seems that women are biblically presented as either the epitome of pure perfection or as degenerate mistresses of evil. It doesn't seem to matter whether they are single or not. But the church's traditional view seems to venerate the family, parenthood and extra-marital chastity in the same way for both sexes.

Suzanne, 28

Jesus gave it a status in a society that wrote women off generally. The whole Bible gives instructions for the care of the widows (presumably single women didn't exist) and there was a duty for the men to look after families, including the women.

Jennifer, 45

Jesus had LOTS of dealings with those I assume were single women: Mary, Martha, Mary Magdalene, etc. etc. Also Lydia and others. Galatians 3:28 applies. We have complementary roles (NOT interchangeable). The men need us. We need the men to complete the image of the church being the bride of Christ. So we need to get on with fulfilling the role that the Lord has given us.

Valerie, 61

I'm not sure that there is anything specifically encouraging women not to be single. Christ revealed himself in the resurrection first to the Marys, and in John's Gospel he stated he was God to a single Samaritan woman first.

Mandy, 34

The Bible doesn't seem as bothered about singleness as an issue as we are today; it's more concerned with lifestyle (which I think encompasses the issue anyway). What I find more interesting is Jesus' treatment and value of single women. All his main women (Martha, Mary, Mary Magdalene) were single. Also, his genealogy includes women who don't fit into the Christian marriage ideal (Solomon's mum, Uriah's wife; Tamar, Judah's daughter-in-law, whom Judah slept with). All this shows that God has a pretty positive view of all women.

Rachel, 25

A few thought the Bible outlined a specific pattern for single womanhood:

> *Purity, a sister and daughter, humble and gentle (nothing very specific). That doesn't mean that we can't be assertive and be business women (see Proverbs 31, last section).*
>
> Imogen, 23

> *One that takes account of Genesis 1 and 2, i.e. made equal but different, and for partnership, not segregation or competition, and Genesis 3 in terms of rebellion and its effects and judgements. The teachings of Paul in 1 Corinthians 7 and 11, 1 Timothy 2 and Titus about how we work out roles in family, church and ministry. A clear understanding of the sovereignty and love of God that the test of his love for me is not whether he gives me a husband but that Jesus died on the cross. That there is a wedding in heaven to which I am invited to meet Jesus the Bridegroom and this is the central relationship of our lives if we are Christian.*
>
> Sandra, 50

> *Song of Songs is helpful when it advises the young virgins of Jerusalem: 'Do not sir up or awaken love until it is ready' – encouraging a patient and sober approach to being romantically involved, which many younger Christian women seriously need to adopt.*
>
> Kitty, 21

Jean (53) did not believe that the biblical pattern for single womanhood was different from that of single manhood. 'Why should it be viewed differently for women as for men? she asked. 'Is it because they are expected by society to be mothers and homecarers?' Several women believed that the 1 Corinthians 7 teaching was addressed to men more than it was to women, and that even in the New Testament, marriage was still the preferred status for women.

> *It says far more about men than women, but generally it suggests that women should marry so they can look after their husbands*

*and procreate. Of course, this is in the context of its time and
culture.*

Phoebe, 25

*I can't think of much – women always seem to be married. For
instance, a woman isn't allowed to speak at church, so she should
ask her husband at home – what if she doesn't have a husband? Ruth
got married soon after being widowed, and in the meantime she was
still bound to her mother in the Bible, so I guess we just follow the
general rules given – that you are blessed if you can remain single,
but equally there's nothing wrong with marrying.*

Rhiannon, 20

There was an acknowledgement from several that the Bible's pre-
sentation of single women seems ambiguous: on the one hand,
singleness is promoted, but on the other, marriage is encouraged
for women. Vicky (28) thought the Bible's view of singleness was
'positive', enabling women to be 'more focused on serving the
Lord' and referred to 1 Corinthians 7. Whether one marries is
'up to the sovereignty of God'. Yet she added that the 'normal
path of salvation/life is in marriage and motherhood', citing 1
Timothy 2. Molly (26) agreed:

*I think there are conflicting biblical views of single women. Paul
says, 'those that refrain do better!' and yet in Genesis, God says that
it is not good for 'man' to be alone – and makes him a wife. (I believe
that this works for both sexes!) I think generally being part of a
couple seems to be the norm in much of the Bible. Obviously, single
women are meant to be celibate.*

Briony (23) believed that 'the biblical view of women is that they
are all married', adding 'I think it's less acceptable for women to
be single than men'.

The effect of being a Christian on women's views of singleness

When asked the question: 'How does being a Christian affect the
way you view your singleness?' the majority of women felt that

being a Christian gave them a more positive attitude to singleness. They felt God was in control of when and if they were to
marry, and that singleness was therefore a good thing for them at
present. 'I reckon that God's got my future under control,
whether that be being single (and happy in God) or married (and
happy in God),' said Jane (18). Having a relationship with God
provided security, protected them from undue loneliness and
from looking for identity through relationships with men. 'If I
didn't think God was in control of my life and my future, I would
be the world's loneliest person,' reflected Sarah (25). 'I have such
joy and hope and peace in Christ,' said Hilary (55). 'I belong to
him. He is my husband, lover, friend, brother, companion, confi-
dant, mother and father to me.' It enabled them to cultivate a
close relationship with God 'without the interference of other
alliances' (Jean, 53). The consensus was that Christianity was a
major aid to happy singleness. Being a Christian 'validates' singleness (Amy, 28). 'Jesus is the closest person to me,' remarked
Grace (23), 'without that, I don't think I'd last long in my defence
of singleness'.

Negative comments were in the minority. Some women felt
restricted by not being able to date or marry non-Christians. For
Ruth (23), this has been 'inhibiting'. Being unable to marry due
to the lack of Christian men prevented them from having children and from having sexual relationships. 'I shall never have
children of my own and grieve for that,' said Sian (41). 'It's probably a bit scarier than for non-Christians, in that the number of
Christian men is so much smaller than the number of single
Christian women,' said Tanya (25). They felt that because God
had not yet fulfilled their desires for marriage, perhaps he did not
have their happiness in his plans. Although God gives singleness
a status, some said that being in a church whose attitude to singleness was negative caused problems and led to them viewing
their singleness negatively.

*On the one hand, it makes it easier, because the pressure to be in a
relationship is just as intense (although with a different flavour) in
secular society as it is in the Christian ghetto, and if I wasn't a*

Christian and, as a result of my relationship with God, secure and happy in my current marital status, I'd be a bit of a wreck! On the other hand, as a Christian, I do sometimes wonder if it's the ideal to be married and so sometimes I struggle (particularly as if I wasn't a Christian I'd at least be having sex). But forgetting the pressures of others, when it comes down to just me and God, being a Christian gives me a sense of positivity and opportunity in terms of viewing my singleness. It also gives me a sense of security, regardless of my marital status, knowing the depth, height, width and breadth (to some small extent) of the love God has for me, which should be the primary source of security for all Christians because you never know what might happen to your partner tomorrow.

Rachel, 25

If I wasn't a Christian, I would have had a sexual history, I would have had the children I so longed for and I wouldn't be so frightened of a lonely future. If you are not seeking a Christian partner, then you still have a chance of new relationships. On a positive note, I am extremely grateful that the Bible gave me a very clear set of rules ... I also believe that life after death will be better.

Jennifer, 45

I am single because of my Christianity! But my faith has helped me also to find great resources when the emotional wells are low. It acts as a touchstone: if the demands of my life become such that I start to feel resentful and bitter at having to bear everything alone, I reduce those demands, instead of wasting away for want of a man. I am also an Oblate of [a convent]. This has helped focus the sacrifice I believe all Christians are called to make. Oblation means 'offering' – and singleness is a special reminder of our offered status as Christians, and our union with Christ for his sake.

Nancy, 45

I feel it is unfair that my non-Christian friends who are disobeying God and his will get to be happy and in relationships with wonderful men. I find it very difficult, when I am trying to obey God, that I am being punished for my faith by not being allowed to be happy. I am also sick of people telling me I should be happy to be single and they know I am going to find someone – how do they know, when I don't have the first clue?!

Briony, 23

I see my singleness as a calling (for a time at least). Being holy is far more important than being happy, so even if I wasn't happy with it, it wouldn't be a problem. My own view is that if we seek holiness, often God will give us happiness.

Yvonne, 31

Advantages of singleness

When asked about the advantages of being a single Christian woman, the statements 'independence', 'time', 'freedom', 'you can do what you want, when you want', 'more time to spend with others' and 'more time with God' were the most frequently repeated. Being single means a woman is free to make her own decisions without reference to anyone other than God. She is free to travel, work abroad, make her own career choices, and has the flexibility to go wherever God calls her. A single woman can make her own happiness, develop hobbies, and be herself without reference to a man. The extra resources she has by virtue of being without responsibilities for husband or children can be spent in cultivating friendships with other women and men and in serving God and the church.

Freedom, ability to move easily, ability to make decisions without needing to make too many compromises because of family or your husband, more money available both to spend and give away and the freedom to choose between the two. There is a level of friendship that Christian women find with a whole range of people that married folk rarely experience. Being able to be an 'aunt' not just to one's own nephews and nieces but to the children of friends and to enjoy taking children out and being able to send them back afterwards.

Lorna, 51

More time, in theory. Choice of priorities. More room in the bed. No one knows that you've gone to bed early with the cat and a book on New Year's Eve. Freedom from domestic chores – I don't have to cook every night, or complete the ironing. Ability to drop everything for others. Being able to spend time with hurting people without endangering your own relationship.

Jennifer, 45

I have a freedom and carefreeness which many envy. I can pursue my own projects, and be available to people. I can live quite adventurously! – or not. It has given me great opportunities for prayer and contemplation, and an ordered, quiet life, which are biblical goals.

Nancy, 45

Having platonic relationships with men and being able to talk about 'life issues' without strings attached. Focus on God – building on that relationship, rather than a human relationship. Time. Being able to build independent strength.

Cressida, 27

I feel very privileged to have the time and opportunity to look at my relationship with God and revisit the fundamentals of my faith. I feel I have a ministry to my church to help them try to cope with the realities of divorce.

Christine, 54

Independence. Lack of tie to one particular person. Freedom to do what you want when you want. Can alter who you are if you want and act totally out of character. Don't have to take anyone with you when you go out. Can eat what you want (or nothing – if you feel like it!) Can do DIY (feel ashamed of married friends who have to wait till husband gets home so he can fix things for them!) Get the bed all to yourself! Can spend hours being 'girlie'. Don't have to watch football! Can wear whatever you want, don't have to wear what he likes…can be a total slob if you want. Lots of time for other people. Self-reliant … not expecting somebody else to create your happiness. Can choose how to spend your money. Can decide to move house/

decorate without asking anyone else first. Don't have to tidy up after someone else ... in fact don't have to tidy at all if you don't want to! Can get home at whatever time you like – or not at all – without having to check first! Can get so busy that you're never in...and nobody gives you grief about it! Don't have to shave your legs every five minutes! (The list is endless.)

Fiona, 32

Disadvantages of singleness

The women listed marginally fewer disadvantages than advantages to singleness. The overwhelming disadvantage to singleness revolved around the experience of 'loneliness' and 'not having anyone to share with'. Lacking an intimate companion with whom to share the big and the small issues and decisions of life was a significant disadvantage to being single. Singleness brings with it a tendency towards both selfishness and low self-esteem. Single women do not have the opportunity to have children. They sometimes find it difficult to have as active a social life as they would like, due to feeling excluded by married friends. Friends and family may put pressure on them to search for a partner, which leads them to feel stigmatized for being single. They may lack physical affection. Practically, they fear for their physical safety when travelling alone and at night, worry about finances and having to cope alone with DIY jobs and housework. They wish they could form meaningful friendships with both Christian and non-Christian men without the men assuming they regard them as a potential partner.

Loneliness; female friends in couples don't want to share confidences about relationships because they think I won't understand, being single; difficult to deflect unwanted advances; seen as independent-minded; sometimes pitied/matchmade/excluded by couples; maybe girls feel less secure when I'm with their boyfriends; others may think I'm a lesbian, or have something wrong with me, or am a feminist. In general, not too much of a problem.

Imogen, 23

No family excuses to leave the office at a civilized time every evening. No one to share the DIY or housework with. When you buy a home, you don't get the same level of financial support in terms of presents etc. that a newly married couple will get from family and friends. No one to discuss the minutiae of your day with when you get in from work. No one to share the mortgage with and no economies of scale in sharing your life closely with someone. Always having to walk or drive to and from social events on your own, whatever the time of day or night. No meaningful physical affection from one month to the next. No sex. Accepting the fact you may never have children. As a family member by marriage, a partner is better placed than a friend to provide a greater, closer level of practical and emotional support in difficult times, e.g. death of a parent etc.

Sue, 41

Not having someone to spend weekends with/go on holiday with/ share with, feeling left out, loneliness, not having the opportunity to learn from and grow in a close relationship like marriage, having to cook for one when food packaging isn't designed that way!

Jude, 22

No ties! All my close friends have a tendency to go abroad, and I get tired of building good, supportive relationships, and then having to start again when those people move on. The idea of having someone to share life's journey with is very appealing!

Melanie, 26

It can be lonely, isolating, tough on your self-image. As a member of the church, I may be free to serve God, but married people end up with a natural excuse to take time out – single people, on the other hand, don't have to stop at a certain time to meet up with anyone in particular ... and so can get overworked and under-rested. You can also feel on the outside of the church. You don't really belong, and others in the church who are married really don't seem to relate to you. It's quite sad that even as a missionary in my church, I've never had an invitation from anyone to belong to their family, to come around for dinner, or even an invitation just in case I'm not OK at

Christmas etc. By the grace of God, I have good friends, most of whom are single and I do meet up with them on as regular a basis as possible. I guess what the rest of the church sees is a happy person, who is busy doing her work and wouldn't have the time. I know that people are praying for me in the church, which is simply wonderful. But sometimes you just need a little more adoption than that. That's a little sad, isn't it? And if I'm a higher profile person in the church, what of the quiet single woman who comes and sits in church every week in the corner? I guess the disadvantage is that if you want to survive in the church you have to look out for yourself ... because sometimes the church fails to think or take initiative for anyone else. Sounds a little like the world, doesn't it?

Annette, 31

Concluding remarks

Although this research focuses specifically on Christian women, many of its findings concur with those of studies on single women in contemporary society. Studies by Sandra Dalton, Karen Lewis and Sidney Moon, Marcelle Clements, and Tuula Gordon (discussed in Chapter 1) all noted that single women's experiences of singleness are varied. Single women's attitudes to singleness range from the very positive to the very negative. Women's feelings about their singleness tend to change (and sometimes change back again) over the years. Some women become more positive about it; some become more negative; others remain ambivalent.

The majority of women in this study view singleness with mixed feelings. Few are unambiguously negative. Some view singleness positively because they are young and believe they will eventually find a partner. Older women who regard singleness as a good thing have reached this attitude through 'battling' against their own and other people's negative attitudes towards it. The few who see singleness in a predominantly negative light have either not taken up this fighting stance, or feel they have already lost the battle.

The consensus among the women is that being a Christian enables them to view singleness in a more positive light. Their experience of God and, in some cases, their understanding of the Bible, has led them to believe that God is guiding their lives and has their best interests in his plans. However, women's experience of church is problematic, as other Christians are likely to regard singleness as an inferior status to marriage. Some women are pressured by other Christians to find someone to marry. Singleness is rarely given a positive endorsement within evangelical churches. At times, this means that single women are less highly valued in their churches than their married counterparts. As a result, some women have reduced access to roles within their churches. This is compounded by dilemmas about whether women should be accepted into church leadership and preaching roles.

While most women have an adequate social life within their churches, many still experience loneliness and isolation. They have to deal (often alone) with their own emotional reactions to singleness, their desire to marry and issues associated with sex and sexuality. The vast majority want to marry and the lack of Christian men concerns them. While most women view singleness neither as a permanent nor as a particularly positive state, few are actively seeking to escape from it.

5

Theology

Old Testament

For the Jews, marriage and sexual relations were good and were necessary for procreation, companionship and pleasure. Abstinence was unheard of.[1] In the Old Testament, the concept of afterlife was not fully developed. Instead, the emphasis was on immortality through progeny, and having children – male heirs in particular – was crucial. God's covenant promise to Abraham was to occur through Abraham's descendents. Barrenness was regarded as the greatest misfortune.

The Old Testament presents women in relation to men. Where women are single, this is not a desired state. Marriage was more than the norm; it was the requirement. Inger Ljung writes:

An Israelite woman is defined through her relation to a male – she is characterized as wife, daughter, or sister, but also wife-daughter, wife-mother, etc., and sometimes also as concubine or widow; she stands as the object in an overwhelming majority of the references – she is 'taken', 'procured', 'given', or 'received', and she is, above all, a sexual object. If she figures as an acting subject it is generally in contexts telling of the birth of a son.[2]

---

[1] Charles H. Talbert, *Reading Corinthians: A New Commentary for Preachers* (London: SPCK, 1987), 53.
[2] Inger Ljung, *Silence or Suppression: Attitudes towards Women in the Old Testament* (Uppsala, Sweden: Uppsala Women's Studies, 1989), 27.

The woman in Proverbs 31 who is held up as exemplary does not entirely conform to this depiction. She is a strong, wise and hard-working businesswoman. Yet, like the other Old Testament women, she is married and has children. The story of Ruth and Naomi, both widowed women, could be said to provide some validation for singleness: Ruth's willingness to forgo remarriage because of her desire to remain with her mother-in-law Naomi is exalted. Yet remaining single meant destitution, and both women set about to put an end to their poverty. A happy ending is reached when Boaz agrees to marry Ruth and accepts both women into his family.

The understanding that childlessness was a disgrace reappears often in the Old Testament. Psalm 113 praises God that though he is 'high above all nations', he 'looks far down on the heavens and the earth' to the plight of the 'poor' and 'needy'. As an example of how God helps the poor, the psalmist declares 'He gives the barren woman a home, making her the joyous mother of children.' In Isaiah 3:16 – 4:1 God's judgement is prophesied over Jerusalem, who is represented metaphorically as a woman. One manifestation of this judgement will be that the materialistic and proud women's expensive clothes and jewellery will be taken away, their husbands will be killed, and they will beg any surviving men to father children for them, in order that they escape the curse of childlessness.

The role of the eunuch was in existence in ancient Israel. Eunuchs were castrated officials in the royal courts who served the queen or the king's harem. Both Nehemiah and Daniel were likely to have been eunuchs.[3] Some eunuchs enjoyed high political standing, yet their position tended to be ambiguous as their physical impairment resulted in them being scorned and stigmatized by others. Their inability to have children meant that they were viewed with shame and as social deviants. Old Testament law excluded castrated men from the covenant community and

---

[3] David C. Searle, 'Singleness' in David W. Torrance (ed.), *God, Family and Sexuality* (Carberry: Handsel Press, 1997), 96.

from serving as priests.[4] Later in the Old Testament treatment of eunuchs began to point towards Jesus' own teaching. In Isaiah 56:3–5 eunuchs are given a favoured place within God's house:

> Do not let the foreigner joined to the LORD say, 'The LORD will surely separate me from his people'; and do not let the eunuch say, 'I am just a dry tree.' For thus says the LORD: To the eunuchs who keep my sabbaths, who choose the things that please me and hold fast to my covenant, I will give, in my house and within my walls, a monument and a name better than sons and daughters; I will give them an everlasting name that shall not be cut off.

Within the context of Old Testament beliefs about the necessity of marrying and reproducing, God's call to Jeremiah to remain single was highly significant.

> The word of the LORD came to me: You shall not take a wife, nor shall you have sons or daughters in this place. For thus says the LORD concerning the sons and daughters who are born in this place, and concerning the mothers who bear them and the fathers who beget them in this land: They shall die of deadly diseases. They shall not be lamented, nor shall they be buried; they shall become like dung on the surface of the ground. They shall perish by the sword and by famine, and their dead bodies shall become food for the birds of the air and for the wild animals of the earth. (Jer. 16:1–4)

As Craigie, Kelley and Drinkard note, 'Jeremiah's bachelorhood … is so unusual that the Old Testament has no word for a bachelor.'[5] Jeremiah was called to be single as a prophetic sign to his

---

[4] E. Scott Spencer, 'Eunuch', in David N. Freedman (ed.), *Eerdmans Dictionary of the Bible* (Grand Rapids, Michigan: Wm. B. Eerdmans, 2000), 434–5.

[5] Peter C. Craigie, Page H. Kelley and Joel F. Drinkard, *Word Biblical Commentary Volume 26: Jeremiah 1–25* (Dallas, Texas: Word, 1991), 216.

audience that their families would soon be destroyed. R.E. Clements writes:

> Jeremiah was to experience what the men and women of his audience were soon to experience; theirs would be the grief of loss and lamentation for the deaths of mothers, husbands, fathers, and children. His had been the loss dictated by the divine word that he should have no normal family life. In this too he was a paradigm of salvation, sharing fully in the deprivation of those to whom his message was given and declaring that even in the despair engendered by such loss that there still remained hope in the power and renewing of the word of God.[6]

New Testament

Single women in the Gospels

It is necessary to look at the Jewish cultural situation in which Jesus spoke in order to understand the freedom he offered to single women. Jesus' society was strongly influenced by Old Testament ideas about marriage and women. It placed little value on the Enlightenment concept of individuality which is so prized by our own society. The individuality of women was a foreign concept, as was the idea that they could choose the direction their lives took. Instead, the honour and respectability of one's family was all-important. Women were regarded purely in relationship to men, known as 'the daughter of', 'the wife of' or 'the sister of'. They lived in a culture concerned with upholding the values of honour and shame. Ross Saunders defines honour as 'a combination of your assessment of your place in the community plus the community's assessment of your place'. One's degree of honour depended on social status, which was defined by one's family, and people were required to act in accordance with the social position they were born into. Attempts to better oneself

---

[6] R. E. Clements, *Jeremiah* (Atlanta, Georgia: John Knox, 1988), 101.

were frowned upon, unless someone was offered a 'step up' through the patronage of a more highly honoured person. A father was responsible for maintaining the honour of his family, who in turn reflected his honour. A single woman (who would have no honour of her own by virtue of her sex) would have been responsible for maintaining the honour of her male sponsor, who would have been her father, or her brother if her father was dead. Women were required to behave in a modest way, dress demurely, speak to a man only when spoken to, sit in silence at the back of the synagogue and otherwise remain within the home unless accompanied by a man.[7]

Women in Jewish writings were variously described as hardworking, vain, lazy, inclined towards the occult, frivolous, unteachable and likely to lead men into sexual sin. The dominant portrayal of women was as inferior to men. Jewish historian Josephus, who wrote around the time of the early Christians, concluded, 'The woman ... is in all things inferior to a man.' Where women were valued, it was in their capacity as mothers. Judaism placed a high value on marriage and the family. Mary Evans writes, 'It was considered to be essential for a man to marry, and it was the unmarried rather than the married who were seen as unchaste.'[8] Single women, by virtue of their sex and marital status, were a double disgrace.

Jesus treated women as individuals. His disregard for the concepts of honour and shame was subversive and brought dishonour to his family. In the verses directly before his comments on singleness in Matthew 19, he tells his disciples that divorce, permitted under Mosaic law, although expressed differently by the two rabbinical schools of the time, was no longer what he wanted for his followers. At that time, divorce was the prerogative of the man: a wife could not divorce her husband because she was seen as a piece of property owned initially by her father and then by her husband.

---

[7] Ross Saunders, *Outrageous Women, Outrageous God: Women in the First Two Generations of Christianity* (Australia: E. J. Dwyer, 1996), 5–19.

[8] Mary Evans, *Woman in the Bible* (Carlisle: Paternoster, 1998, second edition), 33–35.

Under the school of Rabbi Hillel she could be divorced because she 'displeased' her husband, which could mean if she had broken a dish or was not considered beautiful enough.[9] If a husband divorced his wife, she would lose any children the couple had. Her options were then either to return to her parents' house or to be forced into begging or prostitution.[10] In this context, it is easy to see how Jesus' prohibition against divorce would safeguard against women being regarded as the property of their husbands who could do what they wanted with them.

Jesus' teaching that it was possible to renounce marriage for the sake of the kingdom of heaven was even more subversive. In a culture where women were required to marry or else to face destitution without a male sponsor, he introduced a radical alternative to marriage. Where women refusing to marry would have been objects of shame to their families, Jesus viewed them as women who were putting 'the kingdom of heaven' first. Jewish law had decreed that marriage and parenthood should be every person's priority; one Jewish saying was 'whoever does not think of reproducing himself is like someone who kills his like and the image of God'.[11] Yet Jesus' call to celibacy showed that he valued spiritual reproduction more highly than biological reproduction. Ben Witherington suggests that:

> It was Jesus' teaching on eunuchs for the Kingdom that allowed women to be present among the travelling company of disciples (Lk. 8:1–3), and to remain single and serve the community of faith (Acts 21:9).[12]

---

[9] Carla Ricci, *Mary Magdalene and Many Others: Women who followed Jesus*, trans. Paul Burns (Tunbridge Wells: Burns & Oates, 1994), 65.

[10] Catherine Clark Kroeger, Mary Evans and Elaine Storkey (eds.), *The Women's Study New Testament* (London: Marshall Pickering, 1995), 51.

[11] C. Ricci, *Mary Magdalene and Many Others*, 94.

[12] Ben Witherington, *Women in the Ministry of Jesus* (Cambridge: Cambridge University Press, 1984), 31–2.

Women who chose celibacy were freed from their ties to their households and could thus move around freely wherever Jesus went, provided for by other Christians and by those who welcomed Jesus and his followers into their homes (Lk. 10:7). Single women who moved outside the household structure could gain an identity which was not linked to that of their male relatives.

The Gospels contain several examples of the liberation Jesus brought to single women. Two of these are Jesus' anointing with perfume by a woman known to be a 'sinner' and his visit to the house of Mary and Martha. There are, in fact, several instances of Jesus being anointed by a woman (Mt. 26:6–13, Mk. 14:3–9, Lk. 7:36–50 and Jn. 12:1–8), and these may be varying interpretations of two actual episodes.[13] The fact that all four of the Gospels describe it is a fulfilment of Jesus' declaration 'wherever this good news is proclaimed in the whole world, what she has done will be told in remembrance of her' (Mt. 26:13, Mk. 14:9). By stressing the importance of this woman's adoration of him, Jesus was also ensuring that the episode would remain as an example of the new regard for women that he instituted. The longest version appears in Luke 7:

> One of the Pharisees asked Jesus to eat with him, and he went into the Pharisee's house and took his place at the table. And a woman in the city, who was a sinner, having learned that he was eating in the Pharisee's house, brought an alabaster jar of ointment. She stood behind him at his feet, weeping, and began to bathe his feet with her tears and to dry them with her hair. Then she continued kissing his feet and anointing them with the ointment. Now when the Pharisee who had invited him saw it, he said to himself, 'If this man were a prophet, he would have known who and what kind of woman this is who is touching him – that she is a sinner.' Jesus spoke up and said to him, 'Simon, I have something to say to you.' 'Teacher,' he replied, 'speak.' 'A certain creditor had two debtors; one owed five hundred

---

[13] A discussion of the identity of the women described in the episodes and the similarities and differences in the four accounts can be found in C. Ricci, *Mary Magdalene and Many Others*, 30–31.

denarii, and the other fifty. When they could not pay, he cancelled the debts for both of them. Now which of them will love him more?' Simon answered, 'I suppose the one for whom he cancelled the greater debt.' And Jesus said to him, 'You have judged rightly.' Then turning towards the woman, he said to Simon, 'Do you see this woman? I entered your house; you gave me no water for my feet, but she has bathed my feet with her tears and dried them with her hair. You gave me no kiss, but from the time I came in she has not stopped kissing my feet. You did not anoint my head with oil, but she has anointed my feet with ointment. Therefore, I tell you, her sins, which were many, have been forgiven; hence she has shown great love. But the one to whom little is forgiven, loves little.' Then he said to her, 'Your sins are forgiven.' But those who were at the table with him began to say among themselves, 'Who is this who even forgives sins?' And he said to the woman, 'Your faith has saved you; go in peace.' (Lk. 7:36–50)

Ross Saunders explains that the meal to which the Pharisee invited Jesus was a public affair. The host of such a dinner would publish the guest list beforehand, in order to show that those he was inviting belonged to the same social class, and that he was therefore maintaining the class-based system of honour. The guests would only be men; the women were relegated to the kitchens or to female quarters. Entering the host's house, the men would be kissed. Their feet would be washed and their heads anointed with oil. Because Jesus was of a lower social class, the Pharisee would have instructed his servants not to perform any of these services for him, and to seat him at the bottom of the table.[14]

When Mary enters and ministers to Jesus, she performs for him the three services the Pharisee had deliberately neglected. Jesus explicitly contrasts Mary's actions and faith with that of the male Pharisee. Mary is praised, while the Pharisee is soundly rebuked. It has often been assumed that this woman is Mary Magdalene, and that she was a prostitute. Neither of these assumptions can be

---

[14] R. Saunders, *Outrageous Women, Outrageous God*, 56–7.

proven, but it is possible, given that prostitution was regarded by the Pharisees as a particularly grave sin, and because prostitution was a common profession for single and widowed women unable to otherwise support themselves. That Jesus would speak to, let alone be touched by and forgive, such an 'unclean' woman would have been inconceivable to the Pharisees.[15]

The setting of the story of Mary and Martha, two single sisters, is also domestic.

> Now as they went on their way, he entered a certain village, where a woman named Martha welcomed him into her home. She had a sister named Mary, who sat at the Lord's feet and listened to what he was saying. But Martha was distracted by her many tasks; so she came to him and asked, 'Lord, do you not care that my sister has left me to do all the work by myself? Tell her then to help me.' But the Lord answered her, 'Martha, Martha, you are worried and distracted by many things; there is need of only one thing. Mary has chosen the better part, which will not be taken away from her.' (Lk. 10:38–42)

Martha is rebuked for the priority she gave to domestic service, a traditionally female role, and is told that she should instead have let herself be taught by Jesus. Attention is again drawn to the fact that household codes are being broken, this time initially by Jesus, who enters a house of two single women when there is no sign of their brother Lazarus' presence. This would have been scandalous behaviour. Two men could go alone to the house of one single woman, but a man on his own should not have entered a house occupied only by two single women. Saunders suggests that the reason Martha was so distracted was that she could not bear the shame of the passing neighbours observing Jesus entering the house and teaching her sister. By asking Jesus to tell Mary to help with the domestic work, she was attempting to put an end to the gossip Mary and Jesus' behaviour would have been generating.[16]

---

[15] C. Ricci *Mary, Magdalene and Many Others*, 31.
[16] R. Saunders, *Outrageous Women, Outrageous God*, 40–41.

At that time, the phrase 'to sit at the feet of' meant 'to be a disciple of'. It was used of men being instructed in Judaism by the rabbis; it was never used of women, who were not allowed to become the rabbis' disciples. By allowing Mary and Martha to be his disciples, Jesus was signalling that Christianity would be a religion of male and female equality, where women, and what's more, single women, should be encouraged to learn in the same way men learned. It is possible also that Mary and Martha's single status made it easier for Jesus to teach them: had they had husbands, they might have tried to prevent the women from learning. If this is true, women's singleness would have been an advantage in Christian discipleship. It is clear from the raising of Mary and Martha's brother Lazarus in John 11 that Martha did take up Jesus' challenge to discipleship. This is evident in her understanding of who Jesus is and her declaration, 'I believe that you are the Messiah, the Son of God, the one coming into the world' (Jn. 11:27).

Perhaps the most significant validation of single women is exhibited in the portrayal of Mary Magdalene. Apart from Jesus' own mother, Mary Magdalene appears to be the most significant woman in the four Gospel accounts. She is listed first among the lists of women. She is not defined in relation to male relatives, but solely by the name of her hometown, Magdala. The absence of any information about her family may indicate that she was a single woman. For Mary, like other single women, following Jesus would have brought liberation in her singleness and financial provision from the Christian community.

It is Mary who has the most prominent role as witness to Jesus' resurrection. All the Gospels list women as the first witnesses to and messengers of the resurrection, and Mary Magdalene is the only woman who is named specifically in all four accounts. Indeed, John describes her as being alone at Jesus' first appearance. As Esther de Boer notes, she is not simply a witness; she is 'the key witness'.[17] John writes:

---

[17] Esther de Boer, *Mary Magdalene: Beyond the Myth*, trans. John Bowden (London: SCM, 1997), 46.

Early on the first day of the week, while it was still dark, Mary Magdalene came to the tomb and saw that the stone had been removed from the tomb. So she ran and went to Simon Peter and the other disciple, the one whom Jesus loved, and said to them, 'They have taken the Lord out of the tomb, and we do not know where they have laid him.' Then Peter and the other disciple set out and went towards the tomb. The two were running together, but the other disciple outran Peter and reached the tomb first. He bent down to look in and saw the linen wrappings lying there, but he did not go in. Then Simon Peter came, following him, and went into the tomb. He saw the linen wrappings lying there, and the cloth that had been on Jesus' head, not lying with the linen wrappings but rolled up in a place by itself. Then the other disciple, who reached the tomb first, also went in, and he saw and believed; for as yet they did not understand the scripture, that he must rise from the dead. Then the disciples returned to their homes.

But Mary stood weeping outside the tomb. As the wept, she bent over to look into the tomb; and she saw two angels in white, sitting where the body of Jesus had been lying, one at the head and the other at the feet. They said to her, 'Woman, why are you weeping?' She said to them, 'They have taken away my Lord, and I do not know where they have laid him.' When she had said this, she turned round and saw Jesus standing there, but she did not know that it was Jesus. Jesus said to her, 'Woman, why are you weeping? For whom are you looking?' Supposing him to be the gardener, she said to him, 'Sir, if you have carried him away, tell me where you have laid him, and I will take him away.' Jesus said to her, 'Mary!' She turned and said to him in Hebrew, 'Rabbouni!' (which means Teacher). Jesus said to her, 'Do not hold on to me, because I have not yet ascended to the Father. But go to my brothers and say to them, "I am ascending to my Father and your Father, to my God and your God."' Mary Magdalene went and announced to the disciples, 'I have seen the Lord'; and she told them that he had said these things to her. (Jn. 20:1–18)

In this account, Mary is depicted as a devoted and reliable follower of Jesus. While the other disciples return home, Mary remains weeping at the tomb, such is her devotion to the man who allowed women to become disciples. Her address *'Rabbouni!'* to Jesus indicates the importance of his role as her teacher, and the privilege she had experienced at being one of the first women able to have equal access with men to Christian discipleship.

Jesus commissions her as a witness, telling her to go and report the sighting to his brothers. This, too, was a revolutionary act on the part of Jesus, for in Jewish culture, women were not regarded as reliable witnesses. For a fact to be corroborated, a male witness would be needed. Mark's account demonstrates this point: when Mary tells the disciples that she has seen Jesus, 'they would not believe it' (Mk. 16:11). Mark goes on to note that Jesus 'upbraided them for their lack of faith and stubbornness, because they had not believed those who saw him after he had risen' (Mk. 16:14). The disciples are rebuked for not listening to a single woman whom Jesus had chosen as the first carrier of the message of the resurrection. The centrality of the doctrine of the resurrection to Christianity demonstrates the radical significance of Jesus' choice of a single woman to carry it forward.

In the Gospels, a person's marital status is rarely mentioned. John the Baptist and Jesus were single, and there is no mention of any of the twelve apostles being married, except for Peter, whose marriage we discover when Jesus heals his mother-in-law (Mt. 8:14). Jesus considered people as individuals, rather than in terms of their marital condition. He stated that following him would sometimes necessitate division from and within one's family (Mt. 10:35–39), and that he must always come first. He went even further in subverting the Jewish concept of the sanctity of the family by suggesting that 'whoever does the will of my Father in heaven is my brother and sister and mother' (Mt. 12:50). In presenting himself as the bridegroom coming to marry his bride, the church (Mt. 9:15), he elevates his followers' relationship with him over earthly marriage.

More explicitly, Jesus taught that singleness is a positive way of serving him. According to Matthew:

His disciples said to him, 'If such is the case of a man with his wife, it is better not to marry.' But he said to them, 'Not everyone can accept this teaching, but only those to whom it is given. For there are eunuchs who have been so from birth, and there are eunuchs who have been made eunuchs by others, and there are eunuchs who have made themselves eunuchs for the kingdom of heaven. Let anyone accept this who can.' (Mt. 19:10–12)

Jesus' use of the word 'eunuch' to refer to single people would have been immediately understandable to his audience, given the existence of eunuchs in Jesus' culture. There is some dispute as to whether 'this teaching' (v. 11) which some cannot accept refers to the command against divorce, or to the disciples' comment 'it is better not to marry'. But, either way, the implication is that each state (lifelong marriage or singleness) has been 'given' by God. Each is, therefore, a gift, and singleness is a gift. Furthermore, Jesus describes singleness as a gift irrespective of the circumstances surrounding it and reasons for it. Whether the eunuchs have 'been so from birth', have 'been made eunuchs by others' or 'have made themselves eunuchs', all three have the gift of singleness. To teach that singleness is only a gift in the third case, as some have assumed, would not appear to be a valid argument: in fact, the last group of eunuchs is the group whose situation is the *least* obviously 'given'.

The first two types of eunuch Jesus describes in this passage are those who are single because of circumstance, not because of choice, and he is careful to make it clear that he regards those people's celibacy as just as valuable as that of those who had actively chosen it. These two types of eunuch could today represent women who have not made a particular choice of singleness. There are a variety of reasons for this: perhaps because they have been unable to find a partner, or are attracted to people of their own sex, perhaps because nursing an ill parent prevented them from marrying, or because they were engaged in missionary work on a predominantly female mission field. The third type of single woman is she who has actively chosen not to marry. To all three types of singles, Jesus advocates acceptance of their state.

1 Corinthians 7

Verses 7–9

> I wish that all were as I myself am. But each has a particular gift from
> God, one having one kind and another a different kind.
>
> To the unmarried and the widows I say that it is well for them to
> remain unmarried as I am. But if they are not practising self-control,
> they should marry. For it is better to marry than to be aflame with
> passion.

For Paul, both marriage and singleness are gifts given by God.
After explaining his approval of sex within marriage (7:1–6),
Paul sets out his views on singleness. Paul was 'unmarried' (v. 8).
It is likely that he had at one time been married, due to his probable past occupation as a rabbi and the requirement that all rabbis
should be married. His singleness was therefore likely to have
been due to his wife's death or departure. To those who are
unmarried, he advocates that they stay this way. His statement 'I
wish that all were as I myself am' betrays his strong personal con-
viction of the good of singleness, but he qualifies it by adding
that both singleness and marriage are gifts. 'But each has a particular gift from God' (v. 7) shows that Paul views one's present
marital status as a gift. This is why he counsels the unmarried to
remain as they are (if they can do so without becoming involved
in sexually immoral relationships) and the married likewise to
remain as they are. Remaining unmarried, whether one has never
married or is divorced or widowed (v. 8), is good.

It is necessary to say a word or two about the nature of the
'gift' of singleness, as Paul describes it in verse 7. The Greek word
used for 'gift' (*charisma*) is the same word that is used in the list
of spiritual gifts in 1 Corinthians 12. *Charisma* is also used in
other places in the New Testament such as in Romans 6:23,
where Paul writes 'the free gift of God is eternal life in Christ
Jesus our Lord'. Al Hsu points out that though singleness is a
gift, it is not necessarily a *spiritual gift* in the sense that the 1
Corinthians 12 gifts are. The 1 Corinthians 12 gifts are spiritual

because they carry with them a particular empowerment or anointing which make supernatural an ordinary talent. Hsu notes that the gift of singleness, conversely, is not portrayed as if it is accompanied with a special sense of empowerment. In other words, the gift of singleness is not something which is spiritually discerned. This is an important point, because there is a great deal of misunderstanding about the gift of singleness. Many Christians have come to regard it as an unusual 'calling' or vocation that God supernaturally calls a small and select band of Christians to – perhaps missionaries or those placed by God in unusual situations – and that for the vast majority of Christians, marriage is the ideal situation. Paul's point is, rather, according to Hsu, that singleness:

> is not some supernatural empowerment for some function of ministry. Rather, the gift of singleness is a description of an objective status. If you are single then you have the gift of singleness. If you get married, then you don't. If you marry, you exchange the gift of singleness for the gift of marriedness.[18]

It is just as ridiculous for a single person to deny having the gift of singleness as it is for a married person to deny having the gift of marriage. There is no suggestion either in the text that only a minority of Christians are called to singleness, and that marriage is the best way for the majority of people. Paul does not say what proportion of people God has given the gift of singleness to. Perhaps they *are* a minority, but perhaps in certain situations they will be the majority.

Because Christians have had an incorrect understanding of the gift of singleness, many see singleness not as a gift but simply as a period of waiting for a partner. Singleness has come to be something Christians seek to get rid of, rather than something they wish to rest in, as Paul advocates. This has led to a preoccupation with finding a partner, and a view that anyone who fails to find someone to marry is just that – a failure. The current

---

[18] Al Hsu, *The Single Issue* (Leicester: Inter-Varsity Press, 1998), 61.

imbalance in the number of single Christian men and women has further led women to panic that they will remain 'left on the shelf', and men either to become arrogant because they have so many women to choose from, or to withdraw from the church situation entirely because they cannot cope with the pressure placed on them. Viewing singleness simply as a period of waiting to be married is not only unbiblical, it is also unhelpful for both men and women. Indeed, 80 per cent of single Christian women want to marry, yet the present lack of Christian men means that even if every single Christian man in the UK married one of the still-single women, 50 per cent would still remain unmarried. Given that it is unlikely that every single Christian man will marry, it is probable that only around a third of currently-single Christian women will be able to marry a Christian man. Contemporary Christian misconceptions simply place these women in a limbo state, having neither the gift of singleness nor the gift of marriage. Little wonder that women who have learned to see singleness as a state of waiting rather than a gift are becoming disillusioned with God and, in some cases, leave the church or take non-Christian partners.

Paul's argument that all singles have the gift of singleness is what single Christian women need to hear. They have not been rejected or passed over because they are unattractive, or too independent, or whatever label they have given themselves. Instead, they have been gifted by God. God, who loves to give good gifts to his children (Mt. 7:11), has made them single because he, who loves them most, has their best interests at heart.

In contemporary society, there is seldom a clear line between singleness and marriage: dating and sexual relationships (either casual or serious) occur within the singleness – marriage spectrum. Yet for Paul, there is no such continuum, 'no undefined middle ground between celibacy and the married state'.[19] One is either single (unmarried) or married. As regards sexual behaviour, one is either single and uninvolved in *any* kind of genital

---

[19] John Ruef, *Paul's First Letter to Corinth* (London: SCM, 1971, second edition 1977), 53.

relationship, or married and sexually committed to one's spouse. 1 Corinthians 7 issues a sharp rebuke to contemporary Christian dating practices, in which genital activity of some sort frequently goes on, even if not full intercourse.

While single people are encouraged to remain single, Paul does allow marriage in the case of sexual immorality. Verses 7–9 are parallel with verses 1–2:

> Now concerning the matters about which you wrote: 'It is well for a man not to touch a woman.' But because of cases of sexual immorality, each man should have his own wife and each woman her own husband.

In the case of 'sexual immorality' (v. 2) and 'not practising self-control', it is right to marry. There are several points to make here. First, Paul makes it clear that being single will require one to 'practise self-control': sexual temptation will always be present and desire will need to be restrained. Paul does not mean 'if they are experiencing sexual desire, they should marry'. There is clearly a difference between experiencing desire and committing 'sexual immorality'. Secondly, it is therefore necessary to understand what Paul meant by 'sexual immorality' and 'not practising self-control'. The Greek word for 'sexual immorality' (*porneia*) was explicitly linked to prostitution in the Corinthian context (Corinth was a town with traditional temple prostitution) but other uses in the New Testament show that it refers also to any pre- or extra-marital sexual relationships.[20] The meaning of these verses is that those singles who are indulging in sexual relationships and liaisons would do better to marry. Gordon Fee similarly concludes:

> Paul is not so much offering marriage as the remedy for the sexual desire of 'enflamed youth', which is the most common way of

---

[20] Colin Brown (ed.), *The New International Dictionary of New Testament Theology Volume One* (Exeter: Paternoster, 1976, second edition 1986), 500.

viewing the text, but as the proper alternative for those who are already consumed by that desire and are sinning.[21]

Thirdly, a word about masturbation. Since 'sexual immorality' is sexual activity with a person one is not married to, and given that the Bible speaks nowhere about masturbation, there are no biblical grounds for calling it a sin. It is true that for Christians, sex is not simply a physical gratification of desire but also a profound spiritual and emotional 'one flesh' experience. Masturbation clearly should not be imbued with the significance or the beauty of married Christian sex. While the Bible is positive about married sex, it is simply silent about masturbation. As Stanley Grenz explains, 'The act of masturbation is in itself neither intrinsically moral nor immoral.'[22] The only biblical command which touches on the area of masturbation is Jesus' statement 'everyone who looks at a woman with lust has already committed adultery with her in his heart' (Mt. 5:28). This statement, while about more than simply denouncing lust, prohibits the sexual fantasies which often accompany masturbation. Beyond this, there is no command, which leaves the decision about whether or not to masturbate up to the individual woman. Tony Payne and Phillip Jensen helpfully conclude:

> It is probably best to regard masturbation as a fairly neutral 'coping mechanism' that some individuals may find useful at different times to relieve sexual pressure or frustration. Given the Bible's silence on the subject, it would seem unnecessary to treat masturbation as a 'taboo', or as a matter for guilt.[23]

---

[21] Gordon D. Fee, *The First Epistle to the Corinthians* (Grand Rapids, Michigan: William B. Eerdmans, 1987), 289.
[22] Stanley Grenz, *Sexual Ethics: A Biblical Perspective* (Carlisle: Paternoster, 1998), 215.
[23] Tony Payne and Phillip D. Jensen, *Pure Sex* (Kingsford: Matthias Media, 1998), 98.

Verses 10–11

> To the married I give this command – not I but the Lord – that the
> wife should not separate from her husband (but if she does separate,
> let her remain unmarried or else be reconciled to her husband), and
> that the husband should not divorce his wife.

Although divorce was permissible in Jewish Law, as it is in contemporary Western society, Jesus and Paul did not intend it for
Christian couples. Given the serious view the Bible holds of marriage and its symbolic significance, marriage should not be
entered into unless one is prepared to forgo the possibility of
divorce.[24] That remaining married is hard is the reason why Paul
so emphasizes singleness as an easier way of living. Paul adds
verse 11 in order not to harshly condemn those who have separated or divorced (and in Graeco-Roman culture there was little
distinction between separation and divorce[25]). Rather, he
encourages them to remain unmarried or be reconciled to their
original spouses. He does not say that being reconciled is better
than remaining as they are, as some Christians have imagined
and have condemned outright any divorce or separation. In cases
of domestic violence, for example, there is biblical warrant for
advising the separated or divorced woman to remain unmarried
rather than being reconciled to her husband. Malachi 2:16
shows that in addition to God hating divorce, he also hates
marital violence.[26] Gordon Fee concludes his discussion of verses
10–11 in this way:

> In a culture in which divorce has become the norm, this text has
> become a bone of contention. Some find Paul and Jesus too harsh

---

[24] For a helpful discussion of biblical teaching on divorce and remarriage, see Andrew Cornes, *Divorce and Remarriage: Biblical Principles
and Pastoral Practice* (London: Hodder and Stoughton, 1993).

[25] G. Fee, *The First Epistle to the Corinthians*, 293.

[26] For a helpful discussion of the Christian response to domestic violence, see Helen L. Conway, *Domestic Violence and the Church*
(Carlisle: Paternoster, 1998).

and try to find ways around the plain sense of the text. Others turn the text into law and make divorce the worst of all sins in the church. Neither of these seems an appropriate response. On the one hand, there is little question that both Paul and Jesus disallowed divorce between two believers, especially when it served as grounds for remarriage. Paul does not give reasons for that here, but his view of marriage in Eph. 5:22–23 indicates that it is related to his view of the unitive aspect of marriage and the mutuality of Christian love, which makes it very similar to the reasons Jesus gives.

On the other hand, Paul does not raise this norm to law. Divorce may happen, and such a person is not ostracized from the community. But it must also be remembered that in this setting divorce was being sought for ascetic reasons, which is almost the precise opposite of most such situations in our own culture! What is *not* allowed is remarriage, both because for him that presupposes the teaching of Jesus that such is adultery and because in the Christian community reconciliation is the norm. If the Christian husband and wife cannot be reconciled to one another, then how can they expect to become models of reconciliation before a fractured and broken world?[27]

Verse 24

In whatever condition you were called, brothers and sisters, there remain with God.

As he has done in verse 17 ('lead the life that the Lord has assigned, to which God called you'), Paul in verse 24 stresses God's sovereignty. Verse 24 calls Christians to 'remain with God' 'in whatever condition you were called'. In each case he links their current situation to God's sovereignty: their present marital condition is God's gift to them and is the place where God dwells with them ('there remain with God', v. 24). Roger Ellsworth comments helpfully on the role of God's sovereignty:

---

[27] G. Fee, *The First Epistle to the Corinthians*, 296.

We talk a lot about luck, accidents and chance, but Scripture consistently teaches that God is in control of all things and nothing happens apart from his decreeing or permitting it. The sovereignty of God is a great mystery and our minds are very limited. We aren't able to parcel it out and explain how it all works, but the fact that we cannot understand something doesn't make it false. Don't try to explain the sovereignty of God, but learn to rest in it. When you do you will find contentment. The most difficult and unpleasant situation is transformed by the realization that God, in his sovereign wisdom, has placed us there. If you have trouble accepting the sovereignty of God, think for a while about this: if God isn't in control of every detail, it is sheer folly to talk about trusting him.[28]

Verses 25–31

Now concerning virgins, I have no command of the Lord, but I give my opinion as one who by the Lord's mercy is trustworthy. I think that, in view of the impending crisis, it is well for you to remain as you are. Are you bound to a wife? Do not seek to be free. Are you free from a wife? Do not seek a wife. But if you marry, you do not sin, and if a virgin marries, she does not sin. Yet those who marry will experience distress in this life, and I would spare you that. I mean, brothers and sisters, the appointed time has grown short; from now on, let even those who have wives be as though they had none, and those who mourn as though they were not mourning, and those who rejoice as though they were not rejoicing, and those who buy as though they had no possessions, and those who deal with the world as though they had no dealings with it. For the present form of this world is passing away.

Paul's phraseology 'now concerning virgins' includes virgins of both genders.[29] The passage that follows in fact appears to concern not only virgins, but also other types of single person,

---

[28] Roger Ellsworth, *Strengthening Christ's Church: The Message of 1 Corinthians* (Darlington: Evangelical Press, 1995), 126–7.
[29] C. Talbert, *Reading Corinthians*, 47.

and it has been suggested that the translation 'virgin' would be more accurately rendered 'the unmarried'. Peter Naylor suggests that verse 27 refers specifically to those who are divorced, as the Greek word translated here as 'free' is used of the cutting of a bond.[30] Paul is therefore urging the married not to divorce, and the divorced not to marry. On verse 28 'if you marry, you do not sin, and if a virgin marries, she does not sin', Naylor notes how contrary the Bible's words are to the attitude of today's church:

> This is an extraordinary assertion. No doubt we would say that it must always be preferable for a maiden to marry rather than to remain a permanent spinster. But not Paul. Even in a situation with no marital complications the apostle is less than enthusiastic about a prospective union.[31]

Yet the verse adds the proviso that though singleness is preferable, those who have decided to marry should not be condemned for doing so. Indeed, earlier in the passage Paul noted that marriage is also a gift from God (v. 7). The point is that it is all right to marry; what is inadvisable is *actively* seeking a partner (v. 27). This, again, confronts directly certain contemporary forms of Christian dating.

The rest of the passage presents two principal reasons for staying single. The first is *eschatological* (concerning the end of the world). Paul brings out this point three times: 'in view of the impending crisis' (v. 26), 'the appointed time has grown short' (v. 29), 'for the present form of this world is passing away' (v. 31). Paul viewed the end of the world as imminent. Some commentators have taken the view that Paul has been proved wrong because Jesus has not yet returned and thus should not be listened to on this matter. Yet the authority of Scripture must lead to the conclusion that, whether or not Paul expected Jesus to return in his lifetime, the point is that Christians should be continually expecting Jesus' return.

[30] Peter Naylor, *1 Corinthians* (Darlington: Evangelical Press, 1996), 145.
[31] P. Naylor, *1 Corinthians*, 146.

Expecting the end of the world means that singleness is preferable because marriage only exists in this world. Jesus taught that
there would be no marriage in heaven: 'in the resurrection they
neither marry nor are given in marriage' (Mt. 22:30). No one will
be married to their spouse in heaven. Since marriage is peculiar
to life on earth, and earthly life will shortly be wrapped up, what
is the point of marrying? Paul explains this further by showing
that Christians should make their earthly responsibilities subordinate to their Christian priorities (vv. 29–31). Jerome Murphy-
O'Connor comments that in these verses:

> The vivid phrases cannot be taken literally, but they have to be taken
> seriously. Of course, he expected husbands to continue loving their
> wives. He knew perfectly well that mourners would still weep, just as
> the joyful would still laugh. But Paul wanted to shock people into the
> realization that these were all transitory activities. One should not
> get absorbed in them. Neither pleasure nor pain are permanent, and
> should not determine the way we direct our lives.
>
> What was true on the individual level was also true on the institu-
> tional level. Social and economic systems were no more permanent
> than human emotions. They were already being eaten away by a
> relentless corrosion that could not be reversed. Any serious invest-
> ment in such systems was not only pointless but dangerous. One's
> attention should be focused on the things that really matter.[32]

Paul's main argument is that since earthly priorities are of lesser
importance than heavenly priorities, where is the sense in taking
on marital responsibilities that will make concentrating on God
and eternity more difficult?

Like Jeremiah, whom God called to singleness as a sign to the
people that destruction was on its way, Christian singleness acts
as a prophetic sign that 'the time is short' and Jesus is returning
soon. Christian singles should model their singleness in such a

---

[32] Jerome Murphy O'Connor, *1 Corinthians: The People's Bible Commentary* (Oxford: The Bible Reading Fellowship, 1997, revised edition
1999), 83.

way as to remind the church and to warn the world that judgement is approaching. Jesus cautioned people against becoming like those for whom the future is meaningless and all that matters is marriage. In Luke 17:27 Jesus warns his followers not to be like those in the days of Noah who were 'eating and drinking, and marrying and being given in marriage, until the day Noah entered the ark, and the flood came and destroyed all of them'.

Verses 32–35

> I want you to be free from anxieties. The unmarried man is anxious about the affairs of the Lord, how to please the Lord; but the married man is anxious about the affairs of the world, how to please his wife, and his interests are divided. And the unmarried woman and the virgin are anxious about the affairs of the Lord, so that they may be holy in body and spirit; but the married woman is anxious about the affairs of the world, how to please her husband. I say this for your own benefit, not to put any restraint upon you, but to promote good order and unhindered devotion to the Lord.

The second principal reason for staying single is *practical*. Marriage brings anxiety about 'the affairs of the world' (vv. 33, 34) and Paul wants Christians to exhibit 'unhindered devotion to the Lord' (v. 35). In verse 34 he speaks to both the 'unmarried woman' and the 'virgin'. This offers a sound rebuke to those Christians who have regarded divorce as disqualifying a woman from totally and dedicatedly serving God. Throughout 1 Corinthians 7 demonstrates Paul's sensitivity and inclusivity in those he addresses. He recognizes that never-married and married are not the only marital 'categories', addressing the unmarried (including the divorced), the virgin, the married, the widows, the separated and those married to unbelievers.

In verse 4 Paul writes that a wife is given 'authority' over her husband's body, just as a husband is given 'authority' over his wife's body. Single people, however, are subject only to God. Married people are concerned with 'how to please' their spouses, a focus which is again 'of the world' (vv. 33–34). Singles can be concerned solely about 'the affairs of the Lord' (vv. 32, 34). Single-minded devotion to God, which should be the aim of the single person, has resulted in many single women becoming missionaries and bringing the gospel to many countries and people groups. Yet it is not only freedom for the gospel which singleness brings. Paul's emphasis in this passage is that singleness brings devotion to God and desire for holiness: 'so that they may be holy in body and spirit' (v. 34).

Mary Evans notes that both marriage and singleness are valid states for women. She writes:

> In verse 34, 'the unmarried woman and the virgin are anxious about the affairs of the Lord', Paul shows clearly that he has no time for those who would suggest that the only, or even the proper, vocation for a woman is to be found in marriage and motherhood.[33]

While the single woman is not morally superior to the married woman, there is a sense in which she should be more separated for God's work, more dedicated to him, than the married woman.[34] Spiritual writer Henri Nouwen, a Roman Catholic priest who left an academic career to work with people with mental disabilities, describes singleness (celibacy) as a vital witness for God:

> Celibacy has a very important place in our world. The celibate makes his life into a visible witness for the priority of God in our lives, a sign to remind all people that without the inner sanctum our lives lose contact with their source and goal. We belong to God. All people do. Celibates are people who, by not attaching themselves to any one particular person, remind us that the relationship with God is the beginning, the source, and the goal of all human relationships.[35]

---

[33] M. Evans, *Woman in the Bible*, 72.
[34] P. Naylor, *1 Corinthians*, 149.
[35] Robert A. Jonas (ed.), *Beauty of the Beloved: A Henri J. M. Nouwen Anthology* (London: Darton, Longman and Todd, 1999), 195.

Verse 35 stresses that Paul's advice is intended for the good of his audience. The Greek for 'not to put any restraint upon you' reads literally 'not in order to put a noose around you'. John Ruef comments:

> To tell a person that he is where God wants him to be should, in most cases, be liberating rather than imprisoning. It frees one from the anxiety of wanting always to be somewhere else ... The Corinthians had, in the name of freedom, put the noose around their necks when they failed to relate positively their status in life to their conversion to Christ.[36]

Yet, as he goes on to say in the next verse, and has already said, he is not commanding or enforcing celibacy, simply advocating it as the best choice.

Verses 36–38

> If anyone thinks that he is not behaving properly towards his fiancée, if his passions are strong, and so it has to be, let him marry as he wishes; it is no sin. Let them marry. But if someone stands firm in his resolve, being under no necessity but having his own desire under control, and has determined in his own mind to keep her as his fiancée, he will do well. So then, he who marries his fiancée does well; and he who refrains from marriage will do better.

The reason this section is addressed to men rather than to women is that when the letter was written men had greater responsibility than women in initiating marriage. Ambiguities in the text of verses 36–38 have led to dispute as to whether Paul is addressing men who are contemplating marriage, or the fathers of women contemplating marriage. The majority of commentators have concluded that the verses make better sense read as addressed to engaged men, as the NRSV translation supports. Since this is likely to be an accurate rendering, Paul's argument is very similar

---

[36] J. Ruef, *Paul's First Letter to Corinth*, 66–7.

to that of verses 1–2 and 8–9. 'Not behaving properly' and 'if his passions are strong' points to potential, if not actual, sexual immorality. If such a couple can 'stand firm in ... [their] resolve' and keep their 'desire under control', they should do so and remain single. How far this advice is from that of many Christians today who begin to encourage marriage the moment a couple begin to date. Here, couples in serious relationships are told that 'he who marries his fiancée does well; and he who refrains from marriage will do better'. However, it should be borne in mind that marriages would have been arranged in the Corinthian context, unlike marriages today, which take place when a couple have 'fallen in love' and developed an emotional bond. Paul's advice that engaged couples should consider refraining from marriage may not transcend its cultural context: engaged couples today ending their relationships face an emotional trauma which would have been absent in a situation where marriages were arranged.

Verses 39–40

> A wife is bound as long as her husband lives. But if the husband dies, she is free to marry anyone she wishes, only in the Lord. But in my judgement she is more blessed if she remains as she is. And I think that I too have the Spirit of God.

Christian teaching on marriage is much stricter than was Jewish Law. Verse 39 emphasizes the serious and binding nature of marriage, which helps to explain why it should not be entered into lightly. Since 'a woman is bound as long as her husband lives', when considering marriage she must be very sure that she is willing to undertake such a commitment. If a woman is widowed, she may then remarry, if she so chooses, a man who is a Christian. To marry 'only in the Lord' applies to all categories of single person, echoing Paul's instruction 'Do not be mismatched with unbelievers' (2 Cor. 6:14). Yet although the widow has the option of remarriage, like the other types of single person addressed in 1 Corinthians 7, she is recommended to remain single. The phrase 'she is more blessed if she remains as she is'

(v. 40) reiterates the argument of verses 34–35. The single woman is considered better able to devote herself to God than the married woman, and her decision to remain as she is will enable her to reap the benefits of God's blessings.

The social context

Corinth was a Roman city, and as such, its laws were those of a patriarchal society. Women did not have full legal rights and were subject to a male head of household – usually their father or husband. Only men were able to instigate divorce. In 18 BCE and 9 CE the Emperor Augustus instituted new marriage laws favouring marriage and penalizing anyone who remained unmarried. Marriage was seen as a duty of all Roman citizens. Those who were divorced or widowed were required to remarry within two years of the departure of their previous spouse. Couples who produced children were rewarded; those who did not were subject to sanctions. Despite this law, there is evidence to show that not everyone agreed with or obeyed it. Furthermore, certain upper-class women did achieve relative socio-economic independence. In the Graeco-Roman world, considerable debate took place among the philosophers about the merits and demerits of marriage. The Corinthian church was made up of people from the whole spectrum of Corinthian society, and was thus subject to the debates and ambiguities of that society concerning marriage.

J. Dorcas Gordon explains that Paul's language in 1 Corinthians demonstrates that he saw the Corinthian Christians as belonging to two different kinship groups: their earthly families, in which normal Graeco-Roman bonds were recognized, and the spiritual family, where God was Father and other believers brothers and sisters. Discord may occur when the duties of the two groups conflict: for example, when a woman is seen as subject to her husband under Graeco-Roman customs, yet equal to him as his sister according to Christian teaching. Using a theory developed by anthropologist Victor Turner,[37] Gordon

---

[37] Victor Turner, *The Ritual Process: Structure and Anti-Structure* (Chicago: Aldine, 1969).

reads 1 Corinthians 7 as an example of this conflict between structure (the Graeco-Roman societal obligations) and anti-structure (the equality of all within the Christian community). She concludes that Paul takes a middle line, both upholding the traditional kinship structure and attempting to lessen its hold on Christians.[38] In other words, Paul both upholds and subverts traditional views of marriage, gender and kinship.

Anthropologically, in most cultures gender difference is the primary social distinction. Gender difference is the foundation for institutional, moral and behavioural norms. It is manifested most obviously through marriage, and this has resulted in 'ideal' femininity and masculinity being linked to the roles of wife and husband.[39] Robin Fox lists four rules of kinship which lie at the heart of any society: (1) Women have children; (2) men impregnate women; (3) men usually exercise control; (4) primary kin do not mate.[40] These four rules are fundamentally connected to marriage. Drawing on the findings of other anthropologists, J. Dorcas Gordon describes the effect that advocating singleness has upon a society in terms of its views of marriage and gender identity and roles:

> If singleness and celibacy were to become the ideal form of male/female relationships, the structure of any society would be radically altered. Victor Turner, commenting on how marriage comes under attack in many religious movements, states: 'celibacy becomes the rule and the relationship between the sexes becomes a massive extension of the sibling bond'. Sexual continence neutralizes marriage and family, and, in turn, the statuses and behaviours that specifically pertain to that institution are dramatically altered.[41]

---

[38] J. Dorcas Gordon, *Sister or Wife?: 1 Corinthians 7 and Cultural Anthropology* (Sheffield: Sheffield Academic Press, 1997), 69–84, 97–98, 214.

[39] J. Gordon, *Sister or Wife?*, 60–61.

[40] Robin Fox, *Kinship and Marriage: An Anthropological Perspective* (Harmondsworth: Penguin, 1967), 31.

[41] J. Gordon, *Sister or Wife?*, 61.

Whereas women's value had resided largely in their place in their family household, the Bible's approval of Christian single-ness allows women (and men) to gain an identity apart from the household structure. Lisa Sowle Cahill explains that biblical teaching on the significance of singleness has been especially important for women:

> Unlike their Jewish and Greco-Roman counterparts, Christian women did not have access to the community of faith only through the family, nor was their value defined in terms of procreation of male heirs. While the married life was still acceptable, the sexual subordination of women to men was eroded.[42]

In her study of three celibate communities in nineteenth-century America, Sally Kitch observes similarly that celibacy profoundly alters a community's practice of gender and family life. 'Celibacy ... by eliminating sexual and reproductive relationships, elimi-nates an important premise for the opposition of the sexes', Kitch writes. 'Therefore, although celibacy physically separates men and women, it can actually promote the symbolic unity of the sexes.'[43]

As Gordon's analysis of 1 Corinthians 7 has demonstrated, the Bible both upholds and subverts not only kinship patterns but also traditional gender distinctions. The Old Testament illus-trates that as Judaism developed, male and female roles were increasingly differentiated. Men fought the battles while women looked after the children, and womanhood was explicitly linked to childbearing. Sarah and Hannah cry out to God for freedom from barrenness, which was for women the ultimate disgrace. In the New Testament, gender difference is upheld in the form of marriage, which is defined as a hetrosexual woman-man relationship. Yet, in a fundamental way, Christianity broke many of the Old Testament ideas of gender difference. Gone was

---

[42] Lisa Sowle Cahill, *Sex, Gender, and Christian Ethics* (Cambridge: Cambridge University Press, 1996), 153.
[43] Sally L. Kitch, *Chaste Liberation: Celibacy and Female Cultural Status* (Urbana and Chicago: University of Illinois Press, 1989), 188.

the Jewish practice of allowing women less access to spiritual knowledge or of restricting their place in the Temple: Jesus gave equal support to women and men's spiritual growth. He welcomed the woman with the issue of blood and showed immediate forgiveness to the adulterous Samaritan woman. Gone was the importance of the biological family: all Christians are equally brothers and sisters in Christ. Gone was the association of marriage and motherhood with ideal womanhood: Jesus exalted celibacy as an equally, and in some ways superior, status to marriage. Like Jesus' teaching in Matthew 19, Paul's teaching about the merits of singleness in 1 Corinthians 7, as Ben Witherington explains:

> would have allowed some women the opportunity to establish their own lives and work 'in the Lord' in a way that went against the grain of the patriarchal culture, which liked to keep family property, including female family members, in the hands of one or another male of the family.[44]

The dual project in the New Testament of upholding and subverting difference is also clear in 1 Corinthians 11:2–16. This passage calls for gender distinction to be manifested through dress – in the Corinthian context this was shown by women adopting head coverings and men refraining from wearing them.[45] Yet it also subverts gender distinctions by encouraging women and men equally to pray and prophesy, and by asserting that:

> Nevertheless, in the Lord woman is not independent of man or man independent of woman. For just as woman came from man, so man comes through woman; but all things come from God. (1 Cor. 11:11–12)

---

[44] Ben Witherington, *Conflict and Community in Corinth: A Socio-Rhetorical Commentary in 1 and 2 Corinthians* (Carlisle: Paternoster, 1995), 177.
[45] The Greek 'men' and 'women' could be equally rendered 'husbands' and 'wives'.

Applying the insights gained from anthropological under-standings of the early Christian community can help to shed light on the present situation. Biblical Christianity will both endorse and subvert gender difference, yet unfortunately many Christians see its project as either to fully uphold or to fully subvert gender difference. Contemporary evangelicalism tends to uphold difference more often than it subverts it, and its idolization of marriage exemplifies this. Could it be, therefore, that God has made such a large proportion of women single in order for a more balanced biblical view to be asserted? Could it be that God's aim through the existence of these single women is to promote singleness as a gift and thereby to re-establish the Bible's neglected element of gender subversion?

As well as challenging traditional stereotypes of gender difference, singleness challenges the Christian definition of 'family'. For Paul, both the church family and the biological family were important. The passage 1 Corinthians 7 pictures the Christian community as in some ways more important than the human family because it will endure into eternity. Applying this to the church today, Ben Witherington writes:

> What is desperately needed and seldom found in the church is an adequate theology of the family of faith. Paul believes that being brothers and sisters in Christ and sons and daughters of God transcends all other loyalties and should transform all other social relationships. Blood should not be thicker than the baptismal waters in the church. Rather Paul calls for a 'relativized' view of all this-worldly institutions, including marriage. His idea of a family 'church' is actualized where God's people treat each other as their *primary* family, not just as some *secondary* social gathering that happens once a week and that promotes the agenda of the nuclear family ... If the physical family will serve the family of faith, that is fine, and it can exist within the *ekklēsia*.[46]

---

[46] B. Witherington, *Conflict and Community in Corinth*, 180.

Given this, could it be that God's other aim, through the proportion of single people in the church today, is to provoke the church to re-establish 'family' primarily as a spiritual category?

There has been much debate as to the status of women and men as we stand between creation and Christ's *re*-creation, between 'nature' and 'grace'. Single Christian women are a battleground upon which takes place a struggle between the now and the not-yet, creation and re- or new creation, our present existence and the life to come at the final resurrection. The pattern of womanhood dictated by the creation order, manifest chiefly in the Old Testament and still partially supported in the New Testament, jostles against the womanhood of the new creation, which will be manifest fully at the resurrection, yet has already partially begun. The creation pattern is married and childbearing womanhood. The pattern of the age to come is single womanhood, in which neither marriage nor childbearing will exist. In order to depict correctly to the world this (right) tension between creation and re-creation, both marriage and singleness are necessary and must be supported by the church. If all Christian women were single, the picture of God's creation order would be lost. If all Christian women were married, the picture of the coming new creation would be lost.

It would be legitimate to argue that the often negative attitude to singleness evident in the single women's comments in this book demonstrates that the picture of singleness and the new creation has been eroded, if not lost. This reveals us as a church more concerned with our present existence than with the life to come, with earth than with heaven. Single women have come to stand for our disinterest in the things of heaven and for our preference for life in the present. We have stressed Genesis rather than Revelation, creation rather than the age to come. There is discontent among single Christian women who have experienced themselves as uncomfortably regarded because they are (rightly, in biblical thought) out of place with the creation order we have so preferred.

That is why Christians must advocate and support both singleness and marriage. It is not simply that it is wise to teach singleness as a gift because there are more women in the church than men (although this is also a reason for doing so). Rather, there is a profound biblical truth that will not be adequately expressed unless single people are willing to take it on and model it for the church and the world. The gospel's witness will continue to be harmed unless far more people than at present take up the challenge to be willingly single in order to symbolize the coming new creation. They must become signs and symbols of biblical truth. This, I believe, is the theological thinking behind God's regard for the gift of singleness.

Recommendations

Based upon the results of this research, this chapter presents ten suggestions as to how churches can better address single women and the issues they face. These recommendations have been generated from answers given by the women to the question: 'What (if any) improvements should be made in evangelical churches' treatment of single women?'

1 While treating single women as individuals, rather than as a homogenous group, accept and address the variety of issues they face. Consider the different needs of the never-married, the divorced, the separated, the widowed, single parents and those with a non-Christian spouse.

'Single women' may be a category, but single women are not all the same. Each is a unique person made in the image of God with different character traits, backgrounds, life experiences, gifts and skills, and should be treated as such. Having said that, a broad range of issues are associated with the different single marital states which single women may have in common. All must cope in a society and church in which marriage and partnership are more socially acceptable than being single. All must adapt both practically and emotionally to singleness, whether by finding happiness in the single state, or by seeking a partner in order to escape it. Never-married women may think about the prospect of marriage and whether they will enter it. Divorced and separated women have to cope with the emotional scars associated with relationship breakdown and its attendant financial and practical pressures, as do many never-marrieds who have been involved in long-term relationships. Divorced and separated women may be left as single parents, with sole responsibility for financial provision and for nurturing their children. Widowed women, too, may find themselves in this position, as well as dealing with the loss of their most intimate companion. Women married to non-Christian spouses face the ambiguity of being married, yet being unable to share what is most dear to them with their husband. In church environments they are, to all intents and purposes, single. For most women today, singleness is a state of flux and is becoming increasingly hard to define and navigate.

2 Give them a voice within the church and listen to what they say. Value, respect and take them seriously.

Although they make up a quarter of the adult church population, single women tend to lack a voice within the church. This is generally because they rarely hold positions in churches which would enable them to articulate their concerns. If all church decisions are made at an all-male leaders' meeting, there is little chance of single women's voices being heard. A great need in the church today is for single women to be listened to. Listening to women may be instigated by church leaders approaching several single women and asking them to share their wisdom, not simply in dealing with matters to do with women and singleness, but with issues relating to the whole church community. Church decision-making procedures need to involve single women, and it may be necessary to investigate and rearrange local church structures in order to accommodate this.

3 Let them use their wide range of gifts to serve God and the church. Do not simply expect them to take on the jobs no one else wants. Do not discriminate on the basis of marital status.

Allowing single women to speak is likely to open up roles for them in their churches. A woman who shares her concerns about the lack of support for single parents may find herself beginning a single parents' group. A woman who spent her childhood in India may give talks informing the church about issues relating to outreach to Hindus. A woman who is a musician may lead the music group. These are just a few examples of the host of roles potentially available to single women. As adults with unique gifts, single women are gifted to do far more within the church than the children's work and the music group, the most common roles for them currently. Leaders need to expand their vision of the talents of the single women in their congregations and to give them new and increased opportunities to lead and serve. The 50 per cent of churches which do not use single people to lead house groups need to decide to end this discrimination against single people. Character and gifts, rather than marriage, should be what determines who is given leadership responsibilities.

There is a severe lack of single church leaders, as evidenced by Paul Beasley-Murray's research findings, showing that only 4 per cent of church leaders are single. Beasley-Murray's findings also cast doubt on the idea that married men are better suited to leadership. Three-quarters of leaders in his survey reported that pastoring a church had had a negative effect on their wife and children.[1] The current lack of teaching on singleness within churches is likely to be due to the fact that married leaders concern themselves less with issues of singleness than would single leaders. More should be done to encourage single people into church leadership. As those considering church leadership are taught in local churches and theological colleges about the gift of singleness, fewer will view marriage as a necessary prerequisite for leading a church and more will opt to remain single.

4 Address and debate the subject of women's roles in church, and seek to involve single women in leadership.

---

[1] P. Beasley-Murray, *Power for God's Sake*, 27, 39.

The debate about whether or not women can lead churches is far from over, and few Christians have given detailed or informed consideration to the issue. The biblical picture of women's ministry is complex. This makes the issue more, rather than less, important. The equal biblical validity of women's and men's contributions means that the church must seek to understand in what ways women's contributions can be made.

Evidence suggests that women are not faring as well as they could within evangelical churches. Teaching about women's roles is too frequently stated in the negative rather than the positive, listing what it is believed that women cannot do in the church, rather than what they can do. The self-esteem of young Christian women is low. A survey comparing the self-esteem of Bible college students with that of students in secular universities revealed a shocking statistic: 51 per cent of women at mainstream universities, when questioned, said they had above average competence, compared to 58 per cent of men; yet only 31 per cent of female Bible college students responded in this way, compared with 70 per cent of male Bible college students.[2] These figures demonstrate that involvement in at least some of today's evangelical churches increases men's confidence and decreases women's.

Teaching on Christian womanhood has too often equated women with the maternal and wifely function held by only some of them. The 'different' nature of women has been upheld at the expense of equally biblical notions of 'sameness'. For, in truth, women and men are far less different than contemporary Christian stereotypes maintain. Biologically, women are 10–20 per cent shorter, lighter and weaker than men; their sexual organs are different; they have breasts; they can bear children. Numerous academic studies have found that apart from this, differences between the sexes are due to culturally variable patterns of gender, rather than to immutable biological facts. Traditionally 'female' preserves, such as maternal instinct, passivity and

---

[2] Gill Troup, 'Women's Work' *IDEA* March 1999, 21–23.

emotion, have been shown to be socially constructed rather than natural.

Difference-based notions of gender have played a major role in the marginalization of single Christian women. If masculinity is expressed through being a husband and father, a liking for beer, sport and sex and a more rational attitude to the Christian faith, then single men, as well as many other men, have failed. If femininity is equated with wifehood, motherhood, a love of romantic novels and flowers and a more experiential attitude to Christianity, then single women, as well as many other women, have also failed.

So what can be done to redress the balance? We must eschew crude gender stereotyping. Mark Greene noted in *Christianity* magazine that if women are those who drive slowly, can't read maps and wear pink, 'it is clear that I am a woman'.[3] For although some of the stereotypes are true for some people, to universalize them is unhelpful. It creates guilt and failure in the woman or man who does not fit the stereotype. A likely consequence of such a discovery is for such a person to attempt to force themselves into a strait-jacket of socially constructed femininity or masculinity which God never intended them to wear. Realizing that they do not fit a gender stereotype may also lead them to question their sexuality. More unites than divides us. We have more in common as human beings than divides us as men and women.

This is not to say that we should reject all concepts of gender difference. As Elaine Storkey explains, the Bible recognizes 'four underlying paradigms which are used interchangeably to describe the relationship between [male and female]'. These are difference, sameness, complementarity and union.[4] There are ways in which men and women are different, the same, complementary and united as bearers of God's image. Neither is it *necessarily* to say that we should dismiss all differentiation in roles

---

[3] Mark Greene, 'Men Behaving Badly', *Christianity* October 2000.
[4] Elaine Storkey, *Men and Women: Created or Constructed? The Great Gender Debate* (Carlisle: Paternoster, 2000), 115–117.

within local churches. It is possible to support male-only elder-ship in churches, yet have women, both single and married, in equal numbers to men serving as deacons, preaching or leading house groups. Male eldership does not necessitate men being more active or authoritative than women in other areas of church life. It should not prevent women from exercising leader-ship gifts or consign them to a subordinate 'helper' role.

There is no biblical reason why single women cannot be on leadership teams. They could take on roles as deacons, pastoral leaders, Bible teachers and house group leaders. They could become youth, student and women's workers. It is time to end the bias against single women that is manifested, for example, in the appointment of youth workers. As Jenny Baker argued in an article on women in youth ministry in *Youthwork* magazine, some female youth workers face discrimination and constraints as they seek to use their gifts within the church.[5] Churches advertising youth worker posts often employ a married man, rather than a single woman. Being married and male are deemed necessary qual-ities in order for a youth worker to understand young people. Yet the problems and compromise which exist in the understanding of singleness and sexual morality among Christians today could be said to result from the lack of singles and women involved in teaching young people. If the only role models available for young people are married men, no wonder Christians are growing up believing that marriage is the most spiritual vocation.

5 Employ single women as pastoral workers and develop female support and mentoring systems, such as women's groups, in which personal issues can be addressed.

The large number of single women in our churches requires that the issues they face are addressed and taught about within the local church. There is a need for a greater number of single female pastors on church leadership teams, women who are qualified to teach about issues such as singleness, sexuality,

---

[5] Jenny Baker, 'Women in Youth Ministry', *Youthwork*, March 2001.

eating disorders, work, depression and responding to societal ideas about women. Too often, the only teaching given to women is conducted by a leader's wife who may have little knowledge or experience of these areas.

In a society which talks much of mentoring, as ours does, Christians would do well to give thought to the issue of role models for single women. Like the historical women Sheila Rowbotham featured in her 1973 study, single evangelical women have largely been 'hidden from history'.[6] Yet there is some record of their existence – for example, in histories of the nineteenth-century feminist and missionary movements. Single women are also present in the biblical narratives, though efforts must be made to bring their neglected stories to light (see Chapter 5). Single women also need single female role models and mentors in their local churches. These mentors need to encourage the development of younger women's individual gifts and talents and to model a vibrant and purposeful single Christian life.

Women need arenas where they can honestly discuss personal issues with other women. While some discussion of this type takes place informally within friendships, there is scope for the establishment of women's (or specifically single women's) groups. Unlike some churches' women's groups, these groups could meet monthly in an evening or at a weekend, in order for single working women to attend.

6 Seek to be a community in which all, single and married, female and male, are involved, loved, supported and needed. Encourage the development of close friendships.

The church needs to revise its idea of what constitutes 'family'. If local churches are modelled on the nuclear family unit, they will perpetuate the sense that the church is an exclusive club for

---

[6] Sheila Rowbotham, *Hidden from History: Rediscovering Women in History from the Seventeenth Century to the Present* (London: Pluto, 1973).

married adults and their two or three children. As was shown in Chapter 5, Jesus subverted the meaning of family, redefining it primarily as a spiritual category. In the gospel, spiritual kinship, more than blood, is what constitutes family, and spiritual reproduction – making disciples of others – becomes more important than biological reproduction.

God's view of family regards and includes each Christian equally, irrespective of their marital status, gender, race or economic status. The family is the whole of God's new covenant people. Etymologically, the noun 'family' derives from the Latin *familia* meaning 'household'. Such a household would have included servants and perhaps members of the extended family, as it would have done in the New Testament church. Though many Christians refer to the church as the 'church family', the New Testament never follows this practice. Instead, it speaks of the church as God's 'household' (Eph. 2:19). As Steve Chilcraft notes, this is 'a much broader term implying the wider, rather than the nuclear, family complete with servants, guests and any other resident. The household of God is *all* who dwell under the same roof.'[7] Returning to this original sense, or instead choosing to speak of the church as a community of believers, would more accurately reflect the New Testament model. In order to avoid the association of the church family with the nuclear family, it may be helpful to speak less of 'family' and more of 'community'. 'Community' is more inclusive, carrying a sense of things held 'in common' by its members. If churches have this view of community, single women will be loved, supported and valued as they are. Marijke Hoek argues that living out church as community is crucial to the well-being of single people:

> The church must be a community whose life together provides and develops true *koinonia*, emotional support and friendships for the singles. Friendship consisting of sharing of lives, expressed in warmth, love and care, provides a rich format for intimacy. The

---

[7] S. Chilcraft, *One of Us*, 82.

church community should not only practise hospitality but also develop wholeheartedly the concept of the family of God.[8]

Singleness should be lived out in community. This is not to say that single people must never live alone, but that friendship through the community of the church is essential. Monks and nuns, who are best known for celibacy, live out their single gift within a wider Christian community. God did not intend singleness to involve loneliness. Instead, it should flourish through the intimacy of friendships. In his book on celibacy, Michael Crosby, a Franciscan and lifelong celibate, says that intimacy with others is needed on three levels: *personal intimacy* (involving mutual disclosure and trust), *sexual intimacy* (involving non-genital yet physical manifestations of care) and *celibate intimacy* (involving spiritual closeness). From these will flow *spiritual intimacy*, 'a relationship of loving closeness and personal familiarity with God that is expressed in compassion for others.'[9] Jesus needed close friendships with other men *and* with women. The Gospel accounts show that he had close relationships with several of his disciples, as well as with Mary, Martha and Lazarus, and with Mary Magdalene.

7 Think through biblical ways in which single women's sexuality can be expressed and celebrated.

Evangelical understandings of sexuality for single people, and especially for single women, are woefully inadequate. Instead of seeing sex and sexuality as the preserves of the married, and as

---

[8] Marijke Hoek, 'A New Testament Moral Vision for Singleness', unpublished essay, 2000.

[9] Michael H. Crosby, *Celibacy: Means of Control or Mandate of the Heart?* (Notre Dame, Indiana: Ave Maria, 1996), 147–158, 226. Crosby's choice of the word 'sexual' to refer to non-genital physical intimacy is open to misunderstanding because of our society's equation of sexual intimacy with genital intimacy. 'Sexual intimacy' might be better rephrased as 'physical intimacy'.

aspects of the self which singles must simply repress, Christians need to develop a healthy, biblical and positive view of single sexuality. Greek dualistic thought, which has influenced Western Christianity throughout its history, believed in a division between body and spirit. This concept led to a suspicion of and rejection of the body as a site only of evil and temptation. Yet the Bible is actually very positive about the body. While the body can be used for sin, for Christians, redemption does not occur apart from the body. Philip Sampson describes biblical teaching about the resurrection as:

> not the freeing of the soul from its bodily imprisonment as in Hellenistic thought, nor the mystical flight of an ethereal spirit, but the resurrection of the physical body to a new life on a restored earth. At the centre of the faith is a very material, bodily belief.[10]

Sexuality in the Bible is not simply genital activity. Rather, it is an intrinsic part of the human experience as a man or woman. As Elaine Storkey explains, 'Our sexuality is intrinsically connected to our creaturehood, our bodiliness, but also to our relationality.'[11] Sexuality for single people is to be expressed within the church community. Stanley Grenz describes sexuality as 'the dynamic behind the drive towards bonding in all its forms'. This human desire to bond with others has often been interpreted by single people as desire for marriage, yet singleness is an equally valid arena for bonding to be experienced. The church, in which Christians are bonded or covenanted together as brothers and sisters, is God's primary arena for the expression of single people's sexuality.[12] The failure of some churches to provide for this need is what has led many to view marriage as the source of fulfilment and intimacy.

---

[10] Philip J. Sampson, *Six Modern Myths: Challenging Christian Faith* (Leicester: Inter-Varsity Press, 2000), 118.
[11] Elaine Storkey, 'Spirituality and Sexuality' in David W. Torrance (ed.) *God, Family and Sexuality* (Carberry: Handsel Press, 1997), 153.
[12] S. Grenz, *Sexual Ethics*, 190–193.

Singleness was never meant to be a denial of sexuality, but simply another form of its expression. Sexual intercourse, intended as an expression of the exclusivity of the marriage relationship, has no place in the lives of single people because they have not entered into a marriage covenant. For married people, their relationship with their spouse is where the primary expression of community, gender and sexuality occurs. For single people, their relationships within the church are the main arena for sexual expression. In *God, Sex and Generation X*, Mike Starkey argues that the 'wonder of sexuality' is something which all people need to experience, not simply those who are married. To those who are single he suggests:

> The message to those outside a lifetime covenant relationship is an invitation to intimacy and relationship, no less than to those who are married. But the ways this is expressed will be different. It will involve rediscovering the lost art of vulnerable, self-giving friendship, with people of the opposite sex and the same sex, and rediscovering the touch of affection. Most of all, it will involve learning to be a whole, integrated person, learning the art of cultural resistance in a society which severs body from mind, sexuality from commitment.[13]

8 Do not put marriage on a pedestal. Be honest about its advantages and disadvantages. Do not pressure single women to find partners or make them feel as if they are second-class because they are single. If couples are dating, do not encourage over-hasty marriage.

In our desire to support 'family values', we have denigrated singleness. We have established a model of relational identity that cripples those who, either by choice or circumstance, do not marry. If Christians are to find their identity and fulfilment in marriage, then single people have failed to achieve wholeness. Furthermore, if gender identity is to be found in marriage, then

---

[13] Mike Starkey, *God, Sex and Generation X: A Search for Lost Wonder* (London: Triangle, 1997), 77–8.

not only have single women failed to attain wholeness, they have also failed to achieve femininity. They are not 'proper' women.

Christians must not imitate society's approval of the nuclear family as the superior marital status. Rather, singles should be encouraged to serve God where they are, free from pressure to marry. Single people's energy is better directed towards serving God than towards searching for a partner. Worshipping marriage, rather than God, is not only idolatrous, it also places an intolerable burden on a marriage partner. Marriage can never bring ultimate fulfilment and risks breaking down when it fails to fully satisfy single people's romantic expectations. Rather, honesty about both the advantages and disadvantages of marriage is needed so that single people are well informed when considering whether and whom to marry. Since 1 Corinthians 7 advises against looking for a partner, Christians should not try to matchmake and should not endorse dating agencies (Christian or otherwise). Instead of encouraging dating couples to marry, the benefits of remaining single should be pointed out, as Paul does in 1 Corinthians 7. It is more justifiable biblically to advise against marriage than to promote it, and the church needs to begin to practise this.

Although Christians seek to protect and cherish the nuclear family, divorce statistics show that Christian marriages break down just as frequently as non-Christian marriages.[14] It is likely that idolizing the institution of marriage does not help it in the long term. If singleness is correctly taught as a gift, people will stop feeling that marriage is a requirement for social acceptability. They will be less hasty in entering marriage and therefore more determined to work at the relationship when they do so. They will be under fewer illusions about its potential as a provider of total fulfilment, and thus less likely to end the relationship when difficulties come. Understood in this light, promoting singleness aids rather than hinders marriage. In *Single: The Jesus*

---

[14] An American survey of 4000 adults in 1999 found that the divorce rate among 'born-again' Christians is higher than for non-Christians. Christian Research *Quadrant,* July 2000.

Model, Heather Wraight quotes an article by John Blatther on how to strengthen Christian marriages. Blatther argues that viewing singleness as a gift will strengthen, rather than weaken, the institution of marriage:

> One of the first things we can do to strengthen Christian marriage is to support singlehood. If people are free to enter marriage wisely, they need to be free of inordinate pressure to escape the single state … We should view singlehood not as a holding pattern for the immature but as a viable option for fruitful Christian life and service. The more viable singlehood is in the church, the fewer bad choices will be made about whether and when and whom to marry.[15]

9 Develop an evangelistic focus on singles in their various states. Bear in mind both the availability of single women to be involved in evangelism, and the need for single men to hear the gospel.

As the proportion of people in society who are single increases, the need to think about evangelism to singles is vital. Instead of focusing evangelistic drives on young families, as the church has tended to do, it is singles to whom the church must now direct its mission. Those Jesus focused on were those who did not fit into the acceptable social moulds, and single people are an obvious example of the sort of people Jesus reached. There is some scope for churches to reach out by running special interest groups, such as divorce recovery groups or lunches for elderly people. Yet for the most part, evangelism to single people does not require particular church-run initiatives: we simply need to go where they are and reach them through friendship. Singles are found in many contexts: they are work colleagues and neighbours; they are members of special-interest groups, such as sports and drama clubs; they are volunteers for charitable organizations. Single

---

[15] John Blatther, 'A Pastoral Strategy for Stronger Marriages' cited in Heather Wraight *Single: The Jesus Model* (Leicester: Crossway, 1995), 33–34.

people are more likely than their married counterparts to engage in hobbies, and a rich source of them is to be found in leisure and voluntary groups.

The recent increase in the proportion of church members who are women does have a bearing on evangelism. In 1979, 55 per cent of the church were women. Ten years later, in 1989, this figure had risen to 58 per cent.[16] The most up-to-date figures put female church membership at between 61 and 65 per cent.[17] While the cry goes out from single women that there are not enough men in the church, the motivation behind this complaint should be other than it currently is. Motivation for preaching the gospel to single men must be the men's need for salvation. Evangelism must be done for the sake of the men themselves, not because single women want Christian spouses.

Yet single women can be powerful tools in the church's evangelistic strategy. The media's portrayal of today's singles is dominated by the Bridget Jones stereotype. Bridget exemplifies societal singles for whom life is disordered and unhappy without a partner. As Chapters 2, 3 and 4 demonstrate, the lives of some Christian singles mirror this depiction. But this should not be the case. Since Christians are called to be different from the world around them, singleness provides an opportunity for Christian women to stand out. Singleness, lived as one of God's gifts, challenges society's ideas about what is important. For Christian singles, hopes of marriage cannot be given first priority; instead, their priority should be to live as worshippers of Jesus. Single women may also be more available to be involved in evangelism: lack of a partner means (in theory, at least) that they have more free time and can be more flexible.

---

[16] P. Brierley (ed.), *Prospects for the Nineties*, 24.
[17] 61 per cent is quoted in Heather Wraight, *Eve's Glue: The Role Women Play in Holding The Church Together*, (Carlisle: Paternoster, 2001), 21. 65 per cent is quoted in Churches Information for Mission, *Faith in Life: A Snapshot of Church Life in England at the Beginning of the 21st Century*, (London: Churches Information for Mission, 2001), 9.

10 Teach both single people and the whole church about the benefits of singleness.

Christian leaders must begin to advocate singleness to their congregations. While there is a temptation to sympathize with those who want to marry but cannot find a partner and to encourage them in their search, to do so is not biblical. Single people need to be taught what the Bible says about the advantages of singleness. Single Christians should be challenged not to reluctantly accept the gift of singleness, but to embrace it.

Since single people make up such a large proportion of the church, singleness needs to be taught about as frequently and in as much detail as is marriage. Teaching could be given in special-interest groups, but it can also be helpful for married people to be present at singleness teaching sessions, in order that they learn better how to treat single people.

Who is to give this teaching on singleness? The primary responsibility for ensuring such teaching is given lies with the church leaders, yet, as shown in Chapter 2, few church leaders teach a biblical view of singleness in their churches. The main forum for teaching on singleness has been Spring Harvest, and local churches need to vocally echo all positive messages given there. If a local church leader feels ill-equipped to conduct such teaching, perhaps because he or she is married, a visiting speaker could be brought in.

Positive teaching about singleness can never begin too early, and children and young people also need to be taught its value. Teaching about sex and relationships in youth groups is too often limited to just that: sex and relationships. Young women may enter adulthood with a biblical perspective on the need to save sex for marriage, but they rarely consider the prospect that they may not marry, because they have not been taught a biblical view of the gift of singleness. It is not until they are in their twenties that the realization dawns that there are far fewer single Christian men than women and that their expectations of marriage may never be fulfilled. By this time, it can be difficult for them to get rid of the mindset which views marriage as a probable, if not definite, part of their future lives.

Convincing Christians of the value of singleness will not be easy, because celibacy runs so counter to the values of society. Yet this makes it all the more vital, for living distinctively Christian lives in an increasingly non-Christian culture demands adherence to a biblical morality of relationships and sexuality. Christian singleness is celibacy. It is not a period of waiting to meet a partner (though marrying is certainly not forbidden), as it is in society as a whole. True Christian singleness is purposeful, unselfish and gospel-centred. It is the dedication of oneself to God without the distraction of a spouse's needs.

In one sense, the aim of this book is to make itself redundant. If we take up the challenge of recognizing singleness as a gift, the Christian media will no longer have to focus their discussions on the dilemma posed by single women. There will be no dilemma, just women and men, single and married, living their lives in the service of the gospel. As one woman wrote to the letters page of *Christianity* magazine, 'If we open our eyes, we'll find in a bizarre sense that we're already married.'[18] The marriage of which she was writing is our marriage to Christ: a marriage that will reach its consummation in heaven, where all talk of earthly marriage, singleness and gender identity will be but a faint memory.

---

[18] 'Say What?', *Christianity*, October 2000.

Appendix 1

What one thing would you like to say to the church about this issue?

Look at what is really happening out there in the community, in the real world.

Christine, 54

Why is it an issue any more than being married? Each has its difficulties and joys.

Fiona, 32

Read the Bible, and stop being pressed into the world's mould, which says that sexual relationships are the key to completeness and happiness.

Sarah, 25

There is an unrealistic assumption that we will become part of a pair. We need to be honest that for most of us this won't happen because there are far more single Christian women than men. Churches feel the need to encourage hope, instead of actually helping with the practical and emotional problem of being single. Please be honest with your flock. Acknowledge that for most of us singleness is not what we would have chosen and it hurts.

Jennifer, 46

Singleness is a choice, *not a disease.*

Mary, 45

We have lost the art of friendship. Increase opportunities for friendship. 'Man was not meant to be alone.' This does not necessarily mean a marriage partner, but companionship. No one is meant to go through life alone.

Andrea, 28

It depends which church. I am aware that some churches, because of their biblical view, think women should not lead or teach. I don't think I agree but I admire their integrity and don't think that criticizing would help, because it is a theological matter.

Becky, 23

If people were encouraged in the single lifestyle, and it was pointed out how much more time you have for ministry opportunities, service at home and away, people might not feel the need to get married so quickly and so young – and, in many cases, so rashly. Marriage and parenthood may bring many joys, but also bring many limits.

Alice, 29

Many people seem to live on the basis of an assumption or a hope that they will eventually get married. This is a shame, because it leaves them thinking that while they're still single they're not complete, while the opportunities for service and Christian development in the context of a single life are enormous.

Carolyn, 23

There is neither ... male nor female. We are all one in Christ Jesus.
Tessa, 26

Use us. We are often financially independent, with a fair bit of free time on our hands to serve the church. We may even own our own homes. Make use of us and our resources, without worrying about pairing everyone off all the time. Do not patronize us, as if we are somehow missing a whole life by not having a husband.

Anna, 26

*It would be great if the church could have consistency in their views
– there seems so much inconsistency within a church. It's fine for
single women to do one thing outside of the church, but within the
church it is a totally different situation. It amazes me that what I do
within the parachurch organization I work for is strongly encouraged by my church, but there is no way I could do what I do within
the church.*

Clare, 29

*Don't discriminate against those who are single either through
choice or lack of opportunity/right person. After all, we are all individuals and God sees us as such, regardless of our marital status.*

Hazel, 32

*We should care for each other first and foremost as brothers and
sisters in Christ. Any other considerations, whilst obviously present
and often important, are surely secondary.*

Catherine, 19

I am too hurt to put it into words.

Jean, 53

*I'd like to see more openness about personal issues within any
marital status group.*

Suzanne, 28

Live love, in sensitivity and support.

Hilary, 55

*We should seek to be inclusive in all our relationships, and not leave
people out from any section.*

Carrie, 30

*Be aware of the struggles and temptations for this group of people,
and try and support and encourage them in the same way you would
married people.*

Eve, 26

Just allow them to be people in their own right. We are not abnormal because we are single; some of us actually prefer it this way (most of the time, at least). Provide good pastoral support for those who struggle with their singleness, and not from the 'we've-been-happily-married-for-fifteen-years' couple in the church!

Yvonne, 31

Most of the people who are preaching about the value of singleness are married, which seems very hypocritical.

Briony, 23

Don't assume every single girl is desperately seeking a husband to feel complete!

Amanda, 29

Acknowledge that being single is more than waiting to get married. I think the church needs to realize that this is a big issue for a large proportion of its members, and it needs to make sure it is addressing it.

Melanie, 26

Romans 12:3–8. Let them belong to the church and be nurtured by it, encouraging them to see singleness not as a nightmare which will one day pass away, but as a gift to be used while God has given it to them.

Annette, 31

Ever thought about arranged marriages?

Alex, 27

Be aware of different needs within the church. For single women to feel that their existence is recognized would be a big help: e.g. the use of illustrations including aunts (who are often significant people in the lives of both children and adults) would actually recognize that they existed.

Lorna, 51

Think, be concerned about individuals, and don't assume everyone is the same.

Jane, 18

Foster sensitivity towards single women, and support them not by isolating and emphasizing their peculiarity, but by including and accepting their value as competent individuals.

Kitty, 21

Respect! Not pity. Paul exalts singleness as a status. We should have the same attitude. It can sometimes feel as though people feel sorry for girls in their late twenties and older who aren't married – what a shame we are still waiting! We need to promote the positives far more. The single men should also learn to take initiative far more.

Vicky, 28

Harness the energy of single women – they want to have more of a role.

Beth, 23

Leave me alone: I'm normal and happy, not desperate for a man to make my life complete.

Denise, 23

Prayer and organized social events.

Sophie, 31

Draw them in, take them seriously, give them value and a role to fulfil. Make them feel needed, in other words. But then we all need that, married or single.

Valerie, 61

Finding a good partner can sometimes seem impossible, but at the end of the day I believe God has it in his hands. But in the meantime, sometimes it seems like a hopeless place to be in your life, and extra support is always welcome (especially from people in the same situation).

Miranda, 20

Treat us as equals, not second-class citizens.

Helen, 44

Is it an issue? Well, if we are a 'group', then use us.

Cressida, 27

We need to accept that there are more female singles than males. Give lessons in female roles in church, singleness and how to survive it, courting/relationships and sexual conduct, in order to give women security and confidence in themselves for their goals as committed Christians.

Frances, 25

Regard them as individuals, without them having to prove their utility, marital status or need first, ensuring inclusion and regular support.

Alison, 20

Singleness is a gift in the same way that being married is. Both are equally valuable, yet wholly different states.

Ruth, 23

Let's go back to the Bible on marriage and relationships and teach biblical principles about marriage and singleness. In particular, we need to work out how to uphold the fact that marriage is great, without teaching that not being married is inferior. Lots of work has gone into understanding and applying what the Bible says on men and women's roles in church life, and in marriage, but I don't think we've paid the same attention to the questions of marriage and singleness.

Annabel, 28

Single women are just as special to God. I would like to see more encouragement – to learn about God, to develop gifts – in order that single women might be fulfilled, but also that they might be taken care of by families within the church, so that loneliness might be less of an issue.

Bethan, 24

It is important to have single people, male and female, in the church, if only to welcome new single people who may be feeling lonely and amazed by the 'couply', family atmosphere. Appreciate us.

Phoebe, 25

Start discussing!

Mandy, 34

Please stop assuming that singleness is a lower state of being than marriage. Stop assuming that we're unhappy all the time. And when we are *unhappy about it, stop telling us we're definitely going to meet someone, just to make us feel better. We* might *not* meet *someone. Encourage us to enjoy where we are, and interact with us so that we can.*

Amy, 28

Preach celibacy as a happy option. Model celibate women i.e. missionary women, Mary Magdalene – women who turned their singleness into an opportunity for God. Affirm single women's gifting – availability, an extra loving heart around the household; encourage what it is they are doing and hold it up for support and prayer. This would get over the suspicion that you are regarded as a slight oddity, or even a failure.

Ensure that marriage is not modelled as the 'perfect way'; there are other ways of being perfect. Jesus chose singleness. We need to ask why, and model our lifestyle on his. Paul preached that for women, remaining unmarried was better. Why? These things are never unpacked. Marriage is also on the political agenda, so the pressure is becoming even greater.

Encourage people to make sure you are invited to Sunday lunch; that you're OK for Christmas, Easter and holidays (all particularly difficult times).

Nancy, 45

It is OK to be single. In fact, Paul recommends it.

Bridget, 43

Not all single women want to get married! There is a role in any church for single people to be single, and to use their gifts as single people. Young people need single role models as much as they need married ones.

Esther, 24

A large percentage of the church is made up of single women. Without us, the church would be depleted. Acknowledge us in a non-patronizing way, and find out how it will benefit the church. In return, we will give you our best.

Moira, 57

Keep praying more for the men of our nation! In almost every Christian situation I am in there are significantly more women than men. Men need to begin to stand up and take their place more, because there is an alarming imbalance in the male: female ratio in the church. Biblical teaching is, of course, essential, but I also think there are too many man-made rules put on the whole 'relationships' issue that somehow make Christian women think that God is just going to present them with the perfect ready-made husband and that they are somehow exempt from the normal real-life process of getting to know someone and the fact that you are not immediately going to 'know'. (I am not talking about the world's confusion and over-emphasis regarding physical compatibility. I respect the suggested physical 'boundaries' but I think that ultimately they should be discussed and decided upon between the two individuals.) People are made so differently, and I do not think we should limit God by being blinkered or afraid of our sexuality. God knows men's hearts, but if we stuck to some of the teaching and guidance on relationships, we would reject outright the chance to get to know a man who wasn't exactly the same kind of Christian as us. It is much easier to make up our own hard and fast legalistic rules than to stick to biblical teaching and remain submitted to God on a daily basis and sensitive to his will in every situation – they are often not as cut and dried as we want to make them.

Cheryl, 24

Don't ignore the issue.

Paula, 28

Allow single women to be honest about wanting a partner and don't devalue, rubbish or dismiss the validity of those feelings or desires. Don't try and super-spiritualize the issue, either.

Sue, 41

Let's empower people to be who God created them to be, unique human beings, whatever their status.

Tamsin, 28

I'm glad that it is OK for women to be vicars now.

Hannah, 28

Get talking! Stop making assumptions about women and talk seriously about the dichotomy that exists between modern women in the workplace and the role of women in the church.

Harriet, 30

Get out there and convert some men!

Tanya, 25

Realize that it is a problem for many people, support them, especially where single people are lonely, pray for them, and be aware of how church often tends to be geared to families.

Molly, 26

Those who are single have as important a role to play in the church as those who are married, and should be treated the same.

Lisa, 31

Be gracious, as Christ is, and continue to obey him and grow more into Christ's likeness.

Imogen, 23

Acknowledge and support us as we try to make some sense of where we fit in the church!

Sian, 41

Do your homework on the teaching on singleness. Don't pigeonhole single women, treating them as a homogenous group, but recognize the different 'states' they are all in. Encourage everyone in their relationship with God, to put God first.

Maggie, 30

Don't make assumptions about single women.

Tina, 35

Single women should be valued as people and members of the body of Christ, just as any other person should be valued. Their gifts should be made use of, as anyone else's gifts would be, within the beliefs of that church (providing they have good biblical foundation).

Nikki, 20

Jesus is not *a consolation prize for the unmarried. We all have a relationship with him; being married or single just adds a different dimension to it. OK!? Grrrrr! (But bless you!)*

Rachel, 25

Appendix 2

Single Women: ten recommendations for the church

1 While treating single women as individuals, rather than as a homogenous group, accept and address the variety of issues they face. Consider the different needs of the never-married, the divorced, the separated, the widowed, single parents and those with a non-Christian spouse.

2 Give them a voice within the church and listen to what they say. Value, respect and take them seriously.

3 Let them use their wide range of gifts to serve God and the church. Do not simply expect them to take on the jobs no one else wants. Do not discriminate on the basis of marital status.

4 Address and debate the subject of women's roles in church, and seek to involve single women in leadership.

5 Employ single women as pastoral workers and develop female support and mentoring systems, such as women's groups, in which personal issues can be addressed.

6 Seek to be a community in which all, single and married, female and male, are involved, loved, supported and needed. Encourage the development of close friendships.

7 Think through biblical ways in which single women's sexuality can be expressed and celebrated.

8 Do not put marriage on a pedestal. Be honest about its advantages and disadvantages. Do not pressure single women to find partners, or make them feel as if they are second-class because they are single. If couples are dating, do not encourage over-hasty marriage.

9 Develop an evangelistic focus on singles in their various states. Bear in mind both the availability of single women to be involved in evangelism, and the need for single men to hear the gospel.

10 Teach both single people and the whole church about the benefits of singleness.

Bibliography

'The Debate', *The Observer*, 5 November 2000

'Say What?', *Christianity*, October 2000

Ainsworth, Claire, 'In sickness and in health', *The Observer*, 5 November 2000

Baker, Jenny, 'Women in Youth Ministry', *Youthwork*, March 2001

Beasley-Murray, Paul, *Power for God's Sake: Power and Abuse in the Local Church* (Carlisle: Paternoster, 1998)

Blatther, John, 'A Pastoral Strategy for Stronger Marriages', cited in Heather Wraight, *Single: The Jesus Model* (Leicester: Crossway, 1995)

de Boer, Esther, *Mary Magdalene: Beyond the Myth*, trans. John Bowden (London: SCM, 1997)

Boseley, Sarah, 'More sex please – we're young, female, liberated and British', *The Guardian*, 30 November 2001

Brierley, Peter (ed.), *Prospects for the Nineties: Trends and Tables from the 1989 English Church Census* (London: MARC Europe, 1991)

Brierley, Peter (ed.), *UK Christian Handbook: Religious Trends 2000/2001 No.2* (London: Christian Research, 1999)

Brown, Colin (ed.), *The New International Dictionary of New Testament Theology Volume One* (Exeter: Paternoster, 1976, second edition 1986)

Cahill, Lisa Sowle, *Sex, Gender, and Christian Ethics* (Cambridge: Cambridge University Press, 1996)

Campbell, Anne, 'Single and over 35? It's a sad, lonely life', *Metro*, 5 March 2001

Carter, Betty, 'Foreword' in Natalie Schwartzberg, Kathy Berliner and Demaris Jacob, *Single in a Married World: A Life Cycle Framework for Working with the Unmarried Adult* (New York: W.W. Norton & Company, 1995)

Central Statistical Office, *Social Focus on Women* (London: HMSO, 1995)

Chandler, Joan, *Women Without Husbands: An Exploration of the Margins of Marriage* (Basingstoke: Macmillan, 1991)

Chilcraft, Steve, *One of Us: Single People as Part of the Church* (Milton Keynes: Nelson Word, 1993)

Chilcraft, Steve, Sheena Gillies and Rory Keegan, *Single Issues: A Whole-Church Approach to Singleness* (Warwick: CPAS, 1997)

Christian Research, *Quadrant*, July 2000

Churches Information for Mission, *Faith in Life: A Snapshot of Church Life in England at the Beginning of the 21st Century*, (London: Churches Information for Mission, 2001)

Clements, Marcelle, *The Improvised Woman: Single Women Reinventing Single Life* (New York: W.W. Norton & Company, 1998)

Clements, R.E., *Jeremiah* (Atlanta, Georgia: John Knox, 1988)

Conway, Helen L., *Domestic Violence and the Church* (Carlisle: Paternoster, 1998)

Coplon, Jennifer Kane, *Single Older Women in the Workforce: By Necessity, or Choice?* (New York: Garland, 1997)

Cornes, Andrew, *Divorce and Remarriage: Biblical Principles and Pastoral Practice* (London: Hodder and Stoughton, 1993)

Craigie, Peter C., Page H. Kelley and Joel F. Drinkard, *Word Biblical Commentary Volume 26: Jeremiah 1–25* (Dallas, Texas: Word, 1991)

Crosby, Michael H., *Celibacy: Means of Control or Mandate of the Heart?* (Notre Dame, Indiana: Ave Maria, 1996)

Dalton, Sandra T., 'Lived Experiences of Never-Married Women', *Issues in Mental Health Nursing* 13 (2) (1992), 69–80

Elderkin, Susan, 'A Mission to Match', *Hotline*, Spring 2001

Ellsworth, Roger, *Strengthening Christ's Church: The Message of 1 Corinthians* (Darlington: Evangelical Press, 1995)

Evans, Claire, 'A Theological Response to the Issues of Singleness within 18–35 year-olds in the Western Church Today', Undergraduate Thesis, London Bible College, 2001

Evans, Mary, *Woman in the Bible* (Carlisle: Paternoster, 1998, second edition)

Fee, Gordon D., *The First Epistle to the Corinthians* (Grand Rapids, Michigan: William B. Eerdmans, 1987)

Fielding, Helen, *Bridget Jones's Diary* (London: Picador, 1997)

Ford, Reuben, Alan Marsh and Louise Finlayson, *What Happens to Lone Parents: A Cohort Study 1991–1995*, Department of Social Security Research Report No.77 (London: The Stationery Office, 1998)

Fox, Robin, *Kinship and Marriage: An Anthropological Perspective* (Harmondsworth: Penguin, 1967)

Frost, Rob, 'You got it Wrong', *Christianity*, August 2000

Gamble, Robin, *The Irrelevant Church* (Eastbourne: Monarch, 1991)

Gerrard, Nicci, 'Will you be lonely this Christmas?', *The Observer*, 12 December 1999

Gibb, Francis, 'Divorce rates fall to lowest for 10 years', *The Times*, 6 December 2000

Gibson, Fiona, 'No Strings Attached' *The Observer*, 18 March 2001

Gordon, J. Dorcas, *Sister or Wife?: 1 Corinthians 7 and Cultural Anthropology* (Sheffield: Sheffield Academic Press, 1997)

Gordon, Tuula, *Single Women: On the Margins?* (Basingstoke: Macmillan, 1994)

Gould, Mary, 'Women on the verge of a brave new world', *The Times*, 18 November 2000

Greene, Mark, 'Men Behaving Badly', *Christianity*, October 2000

Greer, Germaine, *The Whole Woman* (London: Anchor, 2000)

Grenz, Stanley, *Sexual Ethics: A Biblical Perspective* (Carlisle: Paternoster, 1998)

Hartley-Brewer, Julia, 'Brave New Age Dawns for Single Women', *The Guardian*, 18 October 1999

Hill, Amelia, 'Divorce: he's richer, she's poorer', *The Guardian*, 22 October 2000

Hoek, Marijke, 'A New Testament Moral Vision for Singleness', unpublished essay, 2000

Hsu, Al, *The Single Issue* (Leicester: Inter-Varsity Press, 1998)

Jonas, Robert A. (ed.), *Beauty of the Beloved: A Henri J.M. Nouwen Anthology* (London: Darton, Longman and Todd, 1999)

Kay, William K. and Leslie J. Francis, *Drift from the Churches: Attitude toward Christianity During Childhood and Adolescence* (Cardiff: University of Wales Press, 1996)

Keith, Pat M., *The Unmarried in Later Life* (New York: Praeger, 1989)

Kiernan, Kathleen E., 'Who Remains Celibate?', *Journal of Biosocial Science* 20 (3) (1988), 253–263

Kiernan, Kathleen E. and Éva Lelièvre, 'Great Britain', in Hans-Peter

Blossfeld (ed.), *The New Role of Women: Family Formation in Modern Societies* (Oxford: Westview, 1995), 126–149

Kingsley, Lorraine, 'Looking for Mr Right', *Christianity*, June 2000

Kitch, Sally L., *Chaste Liberation: Celibacy and Female Cultural Status* (Urbana and Chicago: University of Illinois Press, 1989)

Kroeger, Catherine Clark, Mary Evans and Elaine Storkey (eds.), *The Women's Study New Testament* (London: Marshall Pickering, 1995)

Lang, Kirsty, 'Bridget Jones – with child', *The Times*, 29 March 2000

Lewis, Karen Gail and Sidney Moon, 'Always Single and Single Again Women: A Qualitative Study', *Journal of Marital and Family Therapy* 23 (2) (1997), 115–134

Ljung, Inger, *Silence or Suppression: Attitudes towards Women in the Old Testament* (Uppsala, Sweden: Uppsala Women's Studies, 1989)

Miller, Naomi, *Single Parents by Choice: A Growing Trend in Family Life* (New York: Plenum Press, 1992)

Naylor, Peter, *1 Corinthians* (Darlington: Evangelical Press, 1996)

Nelsen, Hart M., 'Religious Conformity in an Age of Disbelief: Contextual Effects of Time, Denomination, and Family Processes upon Church Decline and Apostasy' *American Sociological Review* 46 (1981), 632–640

O'Brien, Catherine, 'The Test – Bachelor Girls', *The Times*, 19 July 2000

O'Connor, Jerome Murphy, *1 Corinthians: The People's Bible Commentary* (Oxford: The Bible Reading Fellowship, 1997, revised edition 1999)

Office for National Statistics, *Population Trends Winter 2000 No.102* (London: The Stationery Office, 2000)

Office for National Statistics, *Social Focus on Women and Men* (London: The Stationery Office, 1998)

Office for National Statistics, *Social Focus on Older People* (London: The Stationery Office, 1999)

Office for National Statistics, *Social Trends 30: 2000 Edition* (London: The Stationery Office, 2000)

Office for National Statistics, *Social Trends 31: 2001 Edition* (London: The Stationery Office, 2001)

Page, Nick, 'Single Christian Man: an Endangered Species', *Christianity*, August 2000

Payne, Joan and Martin Range, *Lone Parents' Lives: An Analysis of Partnership, Fertility, Employment and Housing Histories of the*

1958 British Birth Cohort, Department of Social Security Research Report No.78 (London: The Stationery Office, 1998)

Payne, Tony and Phillip D. Jensen, *Pure Sex* (Kingsford: Matthias Media, 1998)

Pollock, Nigel D., *The Relationships Revolution* (Leicester: Inter-Varsity Press, 1998)

Rayner, Jay, 'We want to be alone', *The Observer*, 16 January 2000

Ricci, Carla, *Mary Magdalene and Many Others: Women who followed Jesus* trans. Paul Burns (Tunbridge Wells: Burns & Oates, 1994)

Rowbotham, Sheila, *Hidden from History: Rediscovering Women in History from the Seventeenth Century to the Present* (London: Pluto, 1973)

Ruef, John, *Paul's First Letter to Corinth* (London: SCM, 1971, second edition 1977)

Sampson, Philip J., *Six Modern Myths: Challenging Christian Faith* (Leicester: Inter-Varsity Press, 2000)

Saunders, Ross, *Outrageous Women, Outrageous God: Women in the First Two Generations of Christianity* (Australia: E. J. Dwyer, 1996)

Schwartzberg, Natalie, Kathy Berliner and Demaris Jacob, *Single in a Married World: A Life Cycle Framework for Working with the Unmarried Adult* (New York: W.W. Norton & Company, 1995)

Searle, David C., 'Singleness', in David W. Torrance (ed.), *God, Family and Sexuality* (Carberry: Handsel Press, 1997)

Spencer, E. Scott, 'Eunuch', in David N. Freedman (ed.), *Eerdmans Dictionary of the Bible* (Grand Rapids, Michigan: Wm. B. Eerdmans, 2000), 434–5

Starkey, Mike, *God, Sex and Generation X: A Search for Lost Wonder* (London: Triangle, 1997)

Storkey, Elaine, 'Spirituality and Sexuality', in David W. Torrance (ed.), *God, Family and Sexuality* (Carberry: Handsel Press, 1997)

Storkey, Elaine, *Men and Women: Created or Constructed? The Great Gender Debate* (Carlisle: Paternoster, 2000)

Talbert, Charles H., *Reading Corinthians: A New Commentary for Preachers* (London: SPCK, 1987)

Troup, Gill, 'Women's Work', *IDEA*, March 1999

Turner, Victor, *The Ritual Process: Structure and Anti-Structure* (Chicago: Aldine, 1969)

le Vann, Kate, 'It only takes a fortnight', *Company*, January 2001

le Vann, Kate, 'So, you think you're single?', *Company*, February 2001

Witherington, Ben, *Women in the Ministry of Jesus* (Cambridge: Cambridge University Press, 1984)

Witherington, Ben, *Conflict and Community in Corinth: A Socio-Rhetorical Commentary in 1 and 2 Corinthians* (Carlisle: Paternoster, 1995)

Wraight, Heather, *Eve's Glue: The Role Women Play in Holding The Church Together*, (Carlisle: Paternoster, 2001)

Znaniecka Lopata, Helena, *Current Widowhood: Myths and Realities* (London: Sage, 1996)